Guenter Faltin

Brains versus Capital

Guenter Faltin

Brains versus Capital

Entrepreneurship for everyone

Lean, smart, simple

Picture credit:
illustration p. 84 © Barbara Krafft/Corbis

MIX
Papier aus verantwortungsvollen Quellen
FSC
www.fsc.org
FSC® C110508

German National Library bibliographic information.
This publication is recorded in the German National Bibliography.
Detailed bibliographic information is available via the following internet link: http://dnb.d-nb.de.

www.brains-vs-capital.com

Translator: Lois Feuerle, Portland, OR
Editor: Prof. Fritz Fleischmann, Babson College, Babson Park, MA
Project Management: Florian Komm
Cover design: Barbara Matter & HUNDERTMARK – AGENTUR FÜR KOMMUNIKATION GMBH
Production: Uwe Aufleger, Presse- und Verlagsservice, Erding
Printed by Westermann Druck Zwickau GmbH
Printed in Germany

ISBN 978-3-00-040904-2

Introduction: Why Read This Book?

By Fritz Fleischmann
Babson College

Guenter Faltin, one of the earliest pioneers of entrepreneurship education in Germany, is also the founder of the legendary Teekampagne, a highly unorthodox small company that has become the world's largest importer of Darjeeling tea. His 2008 book, *Kopf schlägt Kapital* (literally: "brains beat capital"), of which the present volume is the authorized translation, is the most successful book on entrepreneurship ever sold in Germany. It has inspired people and changed lives, and its impact continues to grow.

Faced with the growing mountain of books on entrepreneurship, why should you read this one? The answer is simple: because it is so different. So plausible. So helpful. It makes you want to reach for the stars, not for the aspirin.

Mind over Money (as it presents itself to you in English) is a manifesto for people's entrepreneurship, but also a how-to guide on getting started; it is the story of a "radical idealist of capitalism"[1] who shows you how to make money, but who also tells you how to have fun and how to make the world a better place.

Drawing on lessons learned from running his own company and from helping to start a number of others, Faltin demonstrates why a well-thought-out idea is more important than a patent, a new technology, or a large amount of start-up capital. "Concept-creative" thinking, paired with ordinary common sense, is also more important than mastery of business administration subjects – you do not need an MBA or genius-level talent to create a company that beats established competitors in the marketplace. Faltin introduces what he calls the "component principle," a division of labor made possible by the virtual systems of our postindustrial societies: drawing on the experience and the economies of scale of mature companies in specialized areas, you can harness their expertise to your own purposes and focus on the continuing refinement and adjustment of your main idea. Building your start-up from components, you do not need to work yourself to death to be the founder of an enterprise. But you must do your own thinking – something which can be taught and learned, as Faltin demonstrates in his "Labor für Entrepreneurship" in Berlin, a bi-weekly salon that brings together students, founders-to-be, creative intellectuals of various kinds, and interesting individuals who have already taken the leap into successful entrepreneurship. Faltin wants the field of entrepreneurship to re-address, not only in theory but in practice, the Enlightenment's promise of economic self-realization: let us not leave economics to the economists! Let us turn the "dismal science" into a joyful pursuit! And encourage people to participate in this movement.

Getting rich is fun but ultimately pointless, unless it manages to improve something. Faltin's ideal is neither the company man or woman, nor the person who accumulates wealth for the sake of being rich; his ideal is the artist, the creator, the rebel who questions convention and who aims to lead a rich and meaningful life.

This approach keeps alive the connection between business and pleasure, between work and life, between getting and spending. Faltin encourages us to be the entrepreneurs of our own lives: self-determined, rational, passionate, in charge. And this is not an extreme sport either, limited to a few obsessed individuals who are ready to take unusual risks while most of us look on in timid awe. Where many teachers of entrepreneurship favor risk-taking and emphasize "opportunity recognition," Faltin wants us to minimize risk and to avoid the lure of quick opportunities. His is what I call the "slow food" version of entrepreneurship: take your time, prepare well, then sit back and enjoy. Take pleasure in the preparation as well as the eating; enjoy both the work and its rewards. Don't become the slave of your work; keep your head free. Do meaningful work; be mindful of other people and the larger world.

Does this sound impossible? *Mind over Money* shows how it can be done, using the example of the Teekampagne as well as the other successful companies that have been built on the "Faltin model." This model is not just one of the "green shoots of an entrepreneurial spring" breaking out all over the world,[2] but a well-rooted plant from whose seeds other shoots are already growing. Reading this book may well inspire you to plant such a seed and watch it grow into your own tree of life.

Table of Contents

1 Introduction

"All Roads lead to Rome"

This saying from antiquity also applies to the ways to establish a business. However, not all ways are equal. Many seem narrow, mysterious; others appear clear and open. But all of them are difficult and require hard work, or so it is said.

It is striking that along the way you will run across advisers who claim to know the road without ever having traveled it themselves. Even more striking is that when you take a closer look, you find the main route closed. Which of us ordinary mortals starts with a technology patent, research findings or an abundance of capital?

This book describes a road that until now has been little recognized – a road that has more to do with ideas and their development than with research and hi-tech, a road that does not primarily focus on commercial technologies and the quest for capital. A road more compatible with our own times, one could say; one that makes use of the business tools that are available to everyone, one that makes the realm of entrepreneurship accessible to many more people than is the case today. It is a road that makes the figure of the entrepreneur seem closer to that of an artist or composer than to a typical business owner or manager. It is a path that the author himself has traveled and which he describes from personal experience.

And nowadays you can get to Rome more easily and more economically than ever before.

1.1 You've Got to be Crazy

You've got to be crazy if you want to be an entrepreneur: you'll have to work 12 to 14 hours a day, there will be no vacations in the near future, and you'll have little or no private life anymore. You'll be at risk of losing your friends or your life partner to others who are under less stress and have more time. You'll be the first one in the office in the morning and the last to leave at night. You'll have to understand bookkeeping and financial statements. You should have some idea of tax law, business law and labor law, not to mention contract law. You'll have to be able to lead your staff. And be able to talk to and shrewdly negotiate with financial institutions. Naturally you will have to have a good marketing plan, keep your business in good order and make sharp calculations. Risks will come at you, and in droves! Not to mention that your chances of survival in the market are less than 50%. According to many studies, as many as 80% of start-ups have failed by year five at the latest. Thus bankruptcy looms – at least statistically – in return for all your valiant efforts. To put it plainly: in our society with the high level of social entitlements that we have achieved, a person would really have to be crazy to start his own business.

Now there are always people in a society who not only veer off from the mainstream, but who also form an extreme category: alpine mountain climbers who take enormous risks, racing drivers, stuntmen, balloonists like Virgin founder Richard Branson, bungee jumpers, marathon runners, trapeze artists. Start-up entrepreneur: extreme-sport personality with masochistic tendencies?

But our society needs start-up entrepreneurs – and not just a few; to the contrary, we need as many as possible. A kind of people's entrepreneurship. And if this is the case, must we not approach the establishment of start-ups in a way that is totally different from what has been the model up to now? The chapters of this book that follow detail the way out of this malaise. Many of the notions that today still make up the bulk of start-up advice can be tossed aside as easily as you would discard a worn-out toothbrush. We need a radical reorientation. Fortunately many of the latest economic developments dovetail with the very things that we are striving for.

1.2 The Fascination of Economics

Even back in my school days I enjoyed reading about Henry Ford, Andrew Carnegie and Joseph Schumpeter. Not as a class assignment, but reading surreptitiously under my desk. Back when I was in high school, an interest in economics was regarded as something almost disreputable, even indecent. But I could scarcely imagine anything more fascinating and informative. I was raised to be frugal. I didn't spend the first money I earned; instead, I invested it in stock. My parents were shocked, and so were my teachers.

It was obvious that I would study economics. But to my amazement, the subject that had seemed to me so interesting and compelling turned out to be dry and boring at the university. What I had previously experienced as lively and exciting was, as an academic discipline, as lifeless as a cadaver being dissected. Now it is true that the study of medicine does start in the dissecting room, but sooner or later the medical student will work with living people. But with the study of economics, I waited for that in vain. The fascinating figure of the entrepreneur that I had gotten to know with Schumpeter had been replaced by the principle of profit maximization. As a student of economics one is primarily occupied with mathematics and abstract models. I quickly put this kind of academic study behind me, and without the pressure of exams I became even more involved in investigating why a fascinating field like economics became totally lifeless through its study as an academic discipline.

Would anyone ever come upon the idea to teach sports in such a way that the only thing analyzed would be the participants' desire to win? And then to do this using mathematical formulas? With the result that there would no longer be any competition included in the study of physical education, but only mathematics? You laugh? What is taught about competition between companies follows this precise model – starting from the assumption of profit maximization, this formulaic approach with its mathematical models marches into the foreground. It is scarcely possible to find any contact with the living subject embedded in reality. Economics becomes marketing, finance, organization, bookkeeping and accounting. This is the way the cadaver is dissected. The different motives and characteristics of the persons involved no longer exist.

The study of economics from a single perspective diminishes the subject. This is not a matter of whether profit maximization or mathematical formulas are good or bad. The only aspect of interest here is the (unplanned) consequence that not only is the fascination for the subject of economics – which is so central to our society – lost for most students, but it is also lost for the many who would like to use it as a tool.

Now in life it is not unprecedented that someone is called to the very field of endeavor that he had previously criticized so harshly. When a few years later I received an invitation to teach at a university, I swore I would teach economics differently. And how could one do this better than by the example of founding a company?

Me – an entrepreneur? In those days it was difficult to bring these words across my lips. And how to achieve this, pray tell? To get started, don't you need a patent, plenty of capital and, above all, solid economic tools?

That was, in any event, the prevailing wisdom....

2 The Tea Campaign as a Case Study

The concept of the Tea Campaign did not develop overnight. At the beginning it was not at all certain whether the project would involve tea or some other business. I had no firm notions what "my" company would look like. At the beginning my only goal was to combine academic theory with hands-on entrepreneurial practice.[3]

It was like putting together a puzzle, but one whose final result was unknown at the outset and whose individual pieces had yet to be invented.

2.1 The Genesis of the Idea

On my many trips to developing countries it struck me that products like coffee, bananas, sugar and tea cost approximately ten times as much in Germany as they did in their countries of origin. What made these products so expensive here? And why was tea in particular so exorbitantly expensive in Germany, even in comparison to other European countries? Was this attributable to shipping costs, insurance or retailers' high profit margins?

After extensive research it became clear: it was not these costs that made tea expensive, but rather the sheer number of middlemen, plus the small-sized packaging customary in the trade. OK, cut out the middlemen and offer larger, more cost-effective packaging? That seemed reasonable to me, but why wasn't anyone doing it?

Let's take a look at how tea is usually sold in Germany. What makes for a good tea store? It has a good location, friendly and knowledgeable sales help, a pleasant ambiance, and above all, a wide selection of teas. A good tea store carries approximately 150 types of black tea alone, not to mention green teas and a wide variety of flavored teas, such as cherry and passion fruit.

Very quickly this gets the retailer up to several hundred types of tea. When he sells out of one variety, he calls the wholesaler and orders more. The wholesaler in turn purchases from an importer, who buys from an exporter. For orders of three to five kilos, which are customary for retailers, it is impossible to bypass the wholesaler because the order is so small. Much larger quantities are involved at the importer and exporter level.

It is easy to say that you should avoid the middleman, but a conventional business cannot bypass the wholesaler. It simply doesn't make any sense economically. If you want to offer a wide selection, you must keep each variety in stock. If a retailer wishes to purchase directly in the country of origin, he must purchase – and this was borne out by my research – at least two tons of each variety in order to justify the higher shipping costs and the expenditure of bureaucratic time and effort. Thus he would encounter problems with even only 150 varieties. His little shop front would have to have a warehouse the size of a football field behind it.

The Tea Business
(the conventional model)

- ✔ Retail store, good location
- ✔ Broad product range (often several hundred types of tea)
- ✔ Small packages
- ✔ Multiple middlemen necessary (retailer, wholesaler, importer, exporter)

Result:

- ✔ Wide selection
- ✔ High fixed and variable costs
- ✔ Thus, by necessity, higher prices

2.2 Economically Rational Behavior

Still, the idea remained enticing. If one could bypass the middlemen, this would drastically reduce purchasing costs. But as a consequence, if one wanted to behave in an economically rational way, the number of types of tea would have to be limited – significantly.

All right, reduce the product range. But would tea buyers go along with this? After all, customers don't always want to drink the same kind of tea. Would it really be possible to limit the selection? A broad product range is something positive, isn't it? For quite some time now the trend in the tea business has been to create and bring to market ever-new varieties of flavored teas. Anyone who wants to stick with the conventional model for selling tea will not get beyond this.

Nonetheless, I just couldn't let go of the idea that you could offer tea at substantially lower prices if you limited yourself to a few varieties. Yes, simple common sense dictated that it would be most economical to limit yourself radically to a single type of tea. Your purchase quantities would then be large enough for you to buy directly in the producing country, and you would still be able to keep the size of your warehouse within reasonable limits.

2.3 Function, not Convention

Could buyers be induced to forego the multiplicity of teas, select a single variety and then drink it for an entire year? Certainly not! "Only a professor could come up with an idea like that," is what I heard over and over again. For a while it looked as if the idea would fail because of this. If customers are accustomed to being able to make their selection from among many varieties, why should they want to limit themselves so radically? I took a longish breather to think things over.

But I couldn't let it rest. Tea could really be so much cheaper. Moreover, if the purchase price of the tea – which was low in comparison to all the other costs – played only a minor role, then I didn't have to cut corners on the price of the tea I bought. I could purchase an expensive – even a very expensive tea. Yes, why not buy the best tea in the world?

There is such a tea – all the experts agree on this. It grows on the southern slopes of the Himalayas and is named for the region where it is cultivated – Darjeeling. Because I was no tea expert, much less a tea drinker, this is something I learned at the library of the Free University of Berlin. If you could have such an outstanding tea, especially for so little money, perhaps customers would be willing to do without a wide selection. So I thought: as a wine drinker, if I could buy Rothschild Lafite, one of the world's most expensive wines, for the price of an ordinary house wine, then I would only drink Rothschild Lafite.

Limiting the selection to Darjeeling alone had yet another advantage. How was a customer to recognize that my tea really was a much better value? After all, every merchant claims his goods are the best quality at the cheapest price. There has to be a way to make a comparison, and the measuring standard must be well known. Darjeeling is a well-known type of tea and very expensive in the stores. Accordingly, consumers are already familiar with both the quality and pricing for Darjeeling and are thus in a position to make a value-for-money assessment. .

2.4 "Trapped in his Ivory Tower"

The second major cost factor comes from the small packages. Obviously the consumer wants goods that are not spoiled, so small packages are a must. Or are they? What is the shelf life of tea? This is an important question if the consumer is to give up small packages. Even if tea kept its flavor for only one year, that would be long enough if customers bought a year's supply. Then you could sell large packages and see significant savings on packaging materials and packaging expense.

According to legal regulations, tea has a shelf life of three years. Why, then, isn't tea already being sold in large containers? The marketing experts patiently explained that I simply didn't have a clue about actual practice – the average household size in Germany has shrunk, customers are accustomed to small packages and they want 100 grams as the standard. There is even a trend toward supplying 50-gram packages and, yes, even tiny 25-gram cans are being offered successfully with increasing frequency.

I had always been a coffee drinker, and even today I would not want to do without my morning coffee. At one point I realized I was holding a 500-gram bag of coffee in my hand. What? Why is pre-ground coffee, which loses its flavor so much more quickly than tea, sold in packages with a standard weight of 500 grams, while tea is sold in 100-gram packages? This didn't make any sense. Upon closer examination, the standard of 100-gram packages turned out to be mere convention. If you sell ground coffee in 500-gram quantities, then tea can also be sold in packages at least as large.

The Tea Campaign's entrepreneurial risk at the beginning could be boiled down to the question: can consumers be convinced to buy only a single type of tea, and, on top of that, only in large economy-sized packages, if this is rewarded with significant savings? I was sure that we would succeed in convincing customers of the economy, simplicity and rationality of this. But at the beginning I stood totally alone.

My students were dubious when I presented the idea for the first time. "Will we still get our certificates at the end of the semester?" was their first response, referring to the certificate of completion for successful participation in seminars, customary at German universities. (Only practical success would succeed in convincing them.) It was also difficult to find anyone who was willing to sell me tea at all. Most of the exporters I wrote to did not deign to reply; the few who did respond wrote something along the lines of: "Wonderful, Professor, that you want to get hands-on experience, but we highly recommend that you make a little trip to a tea shop to see how tea is actually sold!"

The Tea Business
(an unconventional alternative)

- ✔ Limited to only a single type of tea
- ✔ No middlemen
- ✔ Only economy-sized packages
- ✔ Sales per mail order and Internet

Result

- ✔ Much lower costs,
  resulting in price and quality leadership

2.5 Getting Started Without Money

But there was yet another hurdle: how to finance the project. After all, the first step was a major bulk purchase. In international trade the credit period is 60 days. This meant we had two months before the big bill fell due. The ship from Calcutta to Hamburg takes about four weeks. Once in port at Hamburg, the tea would be unloaded at the Port of Hamburg in two to three days. That left a full month to sell as much tea as possible. Thus the idea of a "campaign". We had to sell fast in order to be able to pay the big bill. The campaign amounted to "Customers, buy your year's supply of tea now that the harvest has landed!" Anyone who wanted to buy tea by mail order had to pay by check in advance. Of course, only an exceptionally attractive offer could induce customers not only to buy large quantities, but also to send their check in advance.

2.6 Clever Concept Offers Many Opportunities

The Tea Campaign had two additional factors built into its concept. In the mid-1980s chemical residues in foodstuffs had for the first time become a matter of great concern to a larger public, as had the relationship of the affluent, industrialized countries with producers in the Third World. Now, it is certainly a good idea for a company to engage and work on the issues that concern the public – and thus its own potential customers. The Tea Campaign did just that by systematically analyzing all its purchases for chemical residues – every single batch, even organic tea – and then buying only those teas with the fewest impurities. Such residue analyses are expensive, and it would increase a conventional tea merchant's costs significantly to undertake them. In the case of the Tea Campaign, however, these costs do not make much of a difference because only one variety of tea is purchased in large volume. Because the test batches are not small, the costs are distributed over large quantities. (The results of the residue analysis, by the way, are disclosed on every package of tea.)

If you achieve your room for economic maneuver through savings on materials, packaging, shipping, and above all by eliminating the middlemen, you don't need to be stingy when it comes to the purchase price of the goods. Thus, unlike others in the tea business who do not command such cost advantages, we don't have to exert pressure on purchase prices in the producing country. These prices are already low, and the producers receive only a small fraction of the high prices consumers have to pay for their tea in western countries. Prices are also low because not all tea described as Darjeeling actually comes from Darjeeling. About 10,000 tons of tea is harvested annually in Darjeeling, but the Tea Board of India estimates that each year 40,000 tons of tea are sold worldwide as Darjeeling. This depresses the prices for the producers. It is especially unfair because Darjeeling's very high altitude and steep slopes make it impossible to produce anything but small harvests. The Tea Campaign concept makes it possible to pay the producers good prices for their Darjeeling tea. We can even afford to provide funding for sustainability projects, primarily through reforestation in Darjeeling, and not on an insignificant scale.

Thus the genius of the Tea Campaign lies in its ability to meld all of the following factors: high quality, decidedly lower prices than the established tea trade, systematic and extensive residue monitoring as well as additional funds for the country of production, and despite this, earn surpluses that stay in the company and represent most of the financing for the company's growth.

Today the Tea Campaign has more than 200,000 customers and sells more than 400 tons of Darjeeling tea a year, and 90% of this is in economy-sized one-kilogram packages.

Since 1996 the Tea Campaign has been Germany's largest mail-order tea business, despite the fact that we handle only one type of tea. According to the Tea Board of India, we have been the world's largest importer of Darjeeling leaf tea since 1998, ahead of even well-known international companies like Lipton, Twinings and Unilever.

How could it be that a ludicrously simple idea (however carefully thought through) has made this company into the market leader? The company's success story cannot be explained using the prevailing doctrine.

Where was the urgent need for capital, which allegedly arises in conjunction with establishing a company? Was the Tea Campaign based on an invention, patent or a brilliant idea? Certainly not. To focus on a single variety of tea is unusual, but it is not an invention. Nor is the principle of economy-sized packaging particularly ingenious.

Were my staff and I good managers and business administrators? No, we were not. In the early years after 1985 the quality of our organization always lagged a year behind where we should have been, given our volume of orders. I remember one day when high up on a top shelf a student found a box containing uncashed checks worth 10,000 German Marks. They had simply been forgotten. But worse yet – no one had even noticed they were missing.

What was crucial, however, was that the basic idea – the puzzle described above, the unorthodox concept that we had thought through so long and so carefully – was so sound that it could withstand even such management disasters.

2.7 The Main Factor Fades into the Background

Can the Tea Campaign's success be explained solely by its specific circumstance? Led by a university professor! Aren't professors, ensconced in their ivory towers, known to be impractical? Was the emerging environmental consciousness of those early years a critical factor? Or did help for the Third World play a central role?

I don't think so. It is true that these factors did attract attention at the beginning, but nowadays the media spotlight fades all too quickly. We cannot and do not wish to compete with so-called modern marketing with its brilliant images and fascinating flair. The idea of helping the Third World certainly brought us sympathy, but at the same time it came with a heavy downside.

It upstaged the Tea Campaign's essential feature – that we could offer the consumer high quality tea at a much lower price than the German tea trade could. After all, Third World projects are known for charging more. You buy there knowing that you are doing good, so you consciously pay a higher price for not necessarily the best quality.

Only gradually was it recognized that the Tea Campaign was apparently achieving the impossible, that is, offering prices that were cheaper by far than in the normal trade, but in spite of this and in addition to this, generating funds for a comprehensive reforestation project. It was as if the spotlight illuminated a minor character but left the leading lady standing in the dark.

Tea Campaign customers who failed to order enough and had to buy their next Darjeeling in tea shops or supermarkets were then astonished at how much money they had to put down at the cash register. The Tea Campaign's long-term success was the result of our outstanding price-performance ratio. This was confirmed by customer feedback as well as by our own customer surveys. As positive as the altruistic element is, and as much a part of the Tea Campaign's identity as it has become, I am sure that our growth would have been far stronger without this aspect.[4] As far as the entrepreneurial concept goes, it placed us in the wrong corner. Our market share of the total tea business in Germany is only about 2.5%. For a company that can convincingly lay claim to price leadership in the market, this is actually a rather meager result.

2.8 The Idea Makes the Difference

It is the quality of the idea that is the decisive factor – an idea that at the outset seemed crazy to almost everyone: only one type of tea and only in big packages. But this was not a whim or a passing fancy; it was a very carefully thought-out concept. The principle is to build from function instead of following convention. If you systematically look for the factors that make a product like tea so expensive in Germany, you almost inevitably come up with this solution. Although it may seem strange, it does make sense because it cuts costs radically. The tea business as it is conventionally run appears to be normal only because this is what we are accustomed to.

Gottlieb Duttweiler, the founder of Migros, the Swiss grocery chain, must have felt the same way. He was amazed at the high prices Zurich retailers were asking for their products. In 1925 he reported that Zurich housewives had to pay three times as much for their purchases as what had been paid in the producing countries.[5] Today this is true to an even greater extent; now the ratio is ten to one. Business costs account for nine tenths of the retail price. Thus, contrary to the generally accepted view, despite all the streamlining, the costs accruing to businesses have risen steeply, particularly due to the ever-increasing expenditures for marketing.

In the work of the psychologist Peter Goebel, we find the first indication that the idea and its development are much more important in starting a business than previously assumed. In his study *Successful Young Entrepreneurs [Erfolgreiche Jungunternehmer]* he analyzed 50 founders of companies who started from a variety of different circumstances. His extensive surveys, including questions about the founders' backgrounds, surprisingly revealed that these founders had only one trait in common: they brought an idea to fruition by persistently addressing the same problem in a way and with a persistence that would appear to a "normal" person to be almost bizarre.[6]

If you examine the individual mental steps that led up to the Tea Campaign, is there even a single step that you yourself could not have taken? I don't see any.

Of course, the Tea Campaign was conceived of as a model for business start-ups, because if I, as a university professor, were to present only theory, that would probably not have been convincing to anyone. The notion that anyone can establish a successful business is just too unusual.

Aristotle said, "Everyone is a philosopher." Joseph Beuys said, "Everyone is an artist." If Beuys sees the capacity for artistic action in everyone, why shouldn't this be even more applicable to entrepreneurial action where the motivation to create an economic perspective on life should be even more compelling? In a kind of expanded definition of the entrepreneur, one could say: "Everyone is an entrepreneur." We must, however, bid farewell to outmoded concepts and identify and endorse the fundamental new conditions for entrepreneurship. But more about that later.

Perhaps you will object, “I can’t afford to buy several tons of a product with the risk that I might ultimately get stuck with it.” This sounds plausible initially, but your fears are unfounded if by means of an unconventional yet cost-saving process you are then able to offer your product considerably cheaper than the market rate. Why, then, should you be stuck with your product? The requirement here is that you continue to think your project through until you find a better, possibly *much* better solution than what is already on the market.

Naturally our concept has been fine-tuned over the years. Today, as the first German company to have entered into a licensing agreement with the Tea Board of India for guaranteed 100% pure Darjeeling, we can trace every crate of tea back to its place of origin, and we have made a name for ourselves for dependable and thorough residue monitoring. Factors like these now make it more difficult for Tea Campaign imitators than was the case previously. Moreover, over the years we have developed a staunch customer base.

Now you may be thinking, yes, all of that will work with a simple product like tea. However, the Tea Campaign’s inherent principle “Function, not Convention” is very useful when it comes to developing *new concepts*, because it calls conventions into question, radically and without any unwarranted respect. For me it was never about tea. I wanted to show that almost everyone is capable of developing an entrepreneurial concept, using his or her everyday knowledge by transferring simple, well-known principles to a new area.

3 Start-Ups: Creative Concepts, Not High Tech

In my professional environment a whole series of new companies has sprung up. They are start-ups trying to build on the foundation of a concept rather than following established wisdom.[7] They start with simple, but well-thought-out and well-developed ideas that require only limited financial resources. They are based on the advantages of a division of labor, if possible creating an entrepreneurial concept out of existing components – principles that I will explain in greater detail in the chapters below. One can think of these new companies as a form of "experimental entrepreneurship" that challenges the common beliefs of how to establish a company by presenting practical alternatives.

3.1 Rethinking the Olive Oil Trade

Artefakt, the company founded by Conrad Boehlicke, applied the Tea Campaign's principles to olive oil, creating an Olive Oil Campaign (www.artefakt.eu). Only through uncompromising quality and the unique character of product and producer is there any chance of competing against fungible, but cheap mass-produced products. By employing the concept of economy-sized packaging marketed directly to the end user, coupled with transparency as to price, cultivation and processing, Artefakt was quickly able to present market alternatives. The company employs a staff of 13 with annual sales of 2.2 million Euro. Thomas Fuhlrott, like Boehlicke a Tea Campaign veteran, founded Zait GmbH, which also deals in olive oil-related products (www.zait.de). Both companies buy their olive oil directly from the producers.

3.2 Rethinking the Conventional Office

Holger Johnson has challenged the conventional view of the office by adopting a functional and thoroughly analytical perspective. Where are costs actually generated? How can existing resources be put to optimal use? A closer look reveals: a large portion of office costs come from the very presence of a secretary. But what exactly does a secretary do? Most secretaries are required to be in the office from nine to five so that they may take incoming phone calls – and rightly so, for calls that go unanswered or are redirected to voicemail not only give the company a bad image, but also cost it lost orders. Holger's research had shown that 2/3 of all callers calling a business did not bother to leave voice mail messages.

However, the time a secretary needs in order to complete her other tasks with concentration is much shorter than the standard nine-to-five. Based upon these considerations, Holger identified two scenarios: Either a secretary is employed full-time simply because someone always has to be there to answer the phone, even though there is, strictly speaking, not enough work to keep her busy for the rest of the time. Or, the secretary is in fact a highly qualified assistant, attending to much more important tasks such as managing business correspondence, preparing presentations or overseeing the post room, but is constantly being interrupted by a ringing telephone. In both scenarios, the secretary is not working to her full potential.

Holger wanted to solve this problem. His ebuero (German acronym for electronic office) created a software which – based on the incoming phone number – identifies which company a caller wants to reach and immediately shows on the computer screen all the pertinent information that company's secretary would usually have on hand. Of course, designing that software was complex and demanding – but it was worth the effort, as it now permits ebuero to serve multiple offices with one secretary, without the callers even noticing that they are actually talking to a service provider. An additional advantage is that ebuero is able to process these calls in a much more professional manner than most companies would be able to do themselves. Because ebuero's secretaries are exclusively employed to handle calls, they fully focus on that single task and receive continuous, high-standard training to further enhance their performance.

And Holger is able to deliver this core office-service for less than ten percent of the conventional cost. He thus found a way to more simply organize the conventional office and to thereby increase its efficiency. ebuero permits businesses to downsize their internal organization by combining, for example, a part-time secretary covering only the main business hours with an ebuero secretary for the rest of the time, or by freeing the assistant from her telephone duties so that she may attend more efficiently to her other tasks for which her physical presence is indispensible.

But ebuero-users do not only save financial costs, but are also relieved of irksome details that require a lot of expertise and extra time. They neither have to find and hire a secretary nor do they have to bother with work contracts or holiday coverage.

Is it easy to find financial backers for such a concept? One would think so, but the reality was quite different. An unconventional idea, untested, unproven – who would want to take the risk? I'm not sure whether I was Holger's first choice as a financier and business angel, but apparently I was the only one willing to embark on this adventure – particularly in the summer of 2000, right in the middle of the Nasdaq crash and the burst bubble of the New Economy. What convinced me in the end was the perseverance and steadfastness with which Holger had fine-tuned his concept for several years and kept on doing so. Holger's success derives from his capacity for conceptual innovation – his willingness to defy convention and put function first. And ebuero has found a noteworthily good way to make its product accessible to interested parties. On ebuero's website www.ebuero.com one can see for oneself how the service works by ordering a free, instant live test. Presently, Holger is giving all aspects of the conventional office a thorough overhaul, thus for a couple of years now, companies in Germany are able to rely on office and conference space ebuero offers for rent in prime locations in a dozen German cities.

To date, ebuero has been copied more than 50 times; yet most of the competitors quickly disappeared from the market and none has been able to match ebuero's success. Why is that? The true strength of a business plan often lies in its attention to detail. Holger is passionate about such details and this is why ebuero, with over 400 employees, is currently Europe's market leader in secretarial services, while Holger himself has been successfully acting as a business angel and mentor for young startups for several years.

An incredible story?

3.3 Rethinking Fruit Juice

You have probably noticed that more than 90% of all the fruit juices you drink are made from concentrate to which the producer has added water. Couldn't you do that for yourself? Of course you could! Then you wouldn't have to pay good money for their expensive water, and you wouldn't have to lug it home with you either. Simply buy the concentrate – preferably in large containers. Yes, you've figured it out. It's the Tea Campaign principle applied to fruit juice. Buy directly at the source if possible – without any middlemen. As in the case of the Tea Campaign, manage the inventory and storage yourself, instead of paying someone else a lot of money to do it for you.

Tap water in Germany is strictly controlled; it is virtually always drinking water of good quality. So is it really necessary to be driving so much water around on German streets and highways? A juice concentrate from which the water has been gently extracted and then replaced by you at home makes good sense economically and ecologically. A pure concentrate without any additives. No sugary soft drinks or colas, no artificial colorings or flavorings. As stipulated for beer by the German Beer Purity Law, only pure ingredients are used – in this case, only fruit and water. An organic option from certified organic cultivation is also possible. No preservatives are necessary because concentrate actually keeps better than juice. The osmotic pressure of concentrated liquids limits the bacteria's ability to attack. Moreover, "bag-in-box" technology prevents air from entering the container once it has been opened, so that the liquid does not come in contact with oxygen, unlike in other bottling processes where air enters the container upon opening, thereby accelerating spoilage and making it necessary to drink the juice quickly. This packaging technology is equally suitable for fresh-pressed juice not from concentrate because that juice, too, will keep longer without preservatives.

The first product introduced by RatioDrink AG (www.ratiodrink.com), the company Rafael Kugel and I established in 2006, was a large three-liter container of apple juice concentrate from the Lake Constance region. For commercial fruit juice the standard is seven to one, that is, seven parts water to one part concentrate. Mixing at home also lets you decide for yourself what degree of concentration suits your taste, as well as whether to mix with tap water, mineral water or something else.

Over and over again we were told that appealing to reason doesn't stand a chance. Emotions, seductive images and clever slogans do a better job of selling. That may be – but perhaps rationality only *appeared* to be difficult to achieve. Accordingly we had to make rational behavior "accessible" – that is, more attractive than the dumbed-down world of modern consumerism. The solution had to be *so* intelligent and *so* economical that it would be easy for our customers to make a rational decision.

This meant painstakingly working it out until all the pieces fit together coherently, until the savings were so great that it was glaringly obvious that with the concept of RatioDrink you would be paying even less for your apple juice than at a discounter. Not to mention that you'd spare yourself transporting all that juice and water, as well as the inconvenience of those empty containers. You'd order the concentrate conveniently on the Internet and get it delivered free to your doorstep.

As for us, the company founders, our workload would also be reduced after the startup phase, so that once again we would be free to pursue new ideas: we ourselves were not involved in any of the steps necessary for producing or shipping the apple juice. We outsourced all necessary services. RatioDrink AG makes use of sector-specific service companies and has spent considerable time identifying good and reliable partners.

If you want apple juice, you have to get apples, press them, collect the juice in containers and ship it. A company near Lake Constance collects the apples throughout the region, processes them into juice concentrate and sends it to our bottler in 1,000-liter tanks. The bottler, in turn, has the task of filling the concentrate into a 3-liter bag-in-box properly, keeping everything clean and sterile. We do not supply this packaging either, but instead purchase it from a manufacturer with the appropriate expertise. After the concentrate is filled into the bag-in-box containers, another company forwards the product to our shipper in Hamburg, who reships it to fulfill our customers' orders. We have also outsourced all the bookkeeping. Thus we don't need to purchase hardware and software for running the company; instead, we delegate the task to someone who does it more professionally and more economically than we could do it for ourselves.

Well, then, how are we spending our time? We have now conceived of an entrepreneurial concept and sought out the proper components to implement it. While others are groaning under their workload, we have time to think about our next steps.

What's new here is that no one had ever bottled juice concentrate in bag-in-box containers. Part of the task, though, was coordinating the producer of the concentrate with our bottler and the packaging manufacturer. Is that all? Not quite. When you use new methods, you can also experience unforeseen problems. The packaging material we used initially proved not to be sturdy enough – it did not always withstand shipment by mail. So implementation has not become less important: the critical issue is that today many operations can be outsourced and placed in professional hands. Recognizing this gave us more freedom to fine-tune the concept instead of having to educate ourselves in a variety of specialty areas.

3.4 Directly to the Chancellor

Caveh Zonooz was working on a number of ideas at once. The first idea he presented to me at the beginning of 2005 was a real estate platform. In the course of more than 20 household moves – his father had to travel a lot – the family learned to mistrust the descriptions provided by real estate brokers. His idea was that it would be better to feature the offered properties on the Internet with realistic pictures and a simple description. Those who were interested could save themselves the expense and inconvenience of traveling to view the properties. I was hesitant because there were already numerous real estate websites on the net.

His second idea, at the beginning of 2006, focused on recording university lectures and then making them available as podcasts. This idea, too, was derived from painful personal experience – Zonooz found it difficult to take notes on the lectures of his professors. Thus the podcasts were to make it possible for students to use the class lectures as an audio book. Whether you are on the bus, jogging or in bed, these days it is easy to take an MP3 player along. Our discussions remained only an exchange of ideas; I did not see a fully developed concept. E-learning makes a lot of promises but keeps very few of them.

Zonooz's third idea, on the other hand, was persuasive. Prominent individuals, so his thinking went, receive many inquiries and are inundated with e-mail. How could one handle this rationally (and economically)? His answer: to take note of all inquiries, but to delegate the work – to the very individuals making these requests. But how could that be done? Everyone sends in their questions. All the questions could be read by the users themselves and evaluated. The prominent individual in question would answer only the inquiries that received the highest ratings. This would mean less work because only a small number of answers would have to be drafted, and those only in a predetermined order. Despite limiting the process to only a few answers, this procedure would be highly representative. And, in the process, it would create an archive of answered questions.

Everyone submitting a question would find out immediately whether or not this or a similar question had already been asked. If the question had been asked, the answer would be instantaneous, but if this were a new question, the questioner would either continue on with the issue, or vote for a similar question that had been formulated in the past.

When Zonooz and his co-founders Alexander Puschkin and Jörg Schiller activated the website www.direktzurkanzlerin.de, they scored a bull's-eye. Twenty days later came the hoped-for letter from the German Federal Press Office. Chancellor Angela Merkel was willing to participate – officially. She would provide three answers each week. This was their breakthrough. The newspaper *Süddeutsche Zeitung* even described the idea as the "Agora[8] of the 21st century."[9] What works for Chancellor Merkel can be adapted for other prominent people or institutions. The idea is scalable.

Then in July 2007 came an inquiry from the USA: Deutsche Welle, the German international broadcasting service, had reported on the concept. The question was: could this software also be used for the US elections? Zonooz and his colleagues were invited to the United States. In Washington, DC, they addressed 200 students. Even the mayor of the capital was fascinated by this innovative idea. In January 2008 came the call from the campaign manager for Senator Barack Obama, candidate for President of the United States. He had heard about the project and felt that it would be a good fit for Obama. In the meantime Straight2who has become a subsidiary of the German company Direktzu GmbH. Their webpage got 500,000 hits in five months. According to *Spiegel online*, the electronic version of the German news magazine *Der Spiegel*, this Internet platform is a rare example of Germany *exporting* a web idea, when otherwise only imitations of successful American platforms are customary in Germany.[10]

In the meantime the Direktzu platform is being used not only by well-known politicians, but also by a number of companies listed on the DAX, the German blue-chip stock market index.

Needless to say, the founders have to keep their minds uncluttered for important decisions. Their time is much too valuable to teach themselves the day-to-day business management skills necessary to run a company. Naturally they have placed bookkeeping and other administrative tasks in the hands of professionals.

Without exception the companies[11] presented here have been successful in the marketplace and have at the same time demonstrated that you can establish a company without focusing on capital resources, operational management or even bookkeeping. These successes suggest that the approach of founding a firm based on an idea, on a concept, may be applicable more widely.

Let us explore this thought further.

4 The Stepchild Concept: It pays to fine-tune your concept

What role does the concept play in founding a company? Neither the research on entrepreneurship nor the practical advice given to startup entrepreneurs places much weight on the underlying idea. Ideas are a dime a dozen. What could an idea be worth anyway?

There is, however, a whole array of very well-known businesses which originated from a new concept. Examples include the German discount supermarket chain Aldi, the Swedish home furnishings company Ikea, Anita Roddick's The Body Shop and Duttweiler's Swiss supermarket chain Migros, not to mention Skype and YouTube. We call them *Concept Creative Startups* because they did *not* spring from a patent, from new research findings or from a new technology, but rather represent a whole new species of business.

The idea itself can be quite simple: Aldi and Ikea each revolutionized their own industry by doing without expensive business furnishings or by having buyers assemble their own furniture. However, those simple ideas usually come at the end of the thought process, rather than at the beginning.

4.1 Not inspirations or passing fancies

When I tell people about the Tea Campaign concept, they often say, "That's so simple! Why didn't I think of that myself?" An understandable reaction. People think it was an idea that was self-evident. Far from it! What looks simple as an outcome was in reality the result of a process that was not at all simple and was often very time-consuming.

When you work tenaciously to achieve a goal, using as few resources as possible, many ideas will gradually be reduced to the essence of their entrepreneurial concept. Just as Picasso was capable of creating a portrait using only a few brush strokes, in the end a good idea may appear as simple as it is masterful. But as a rule, getting there has taken you through protracted thought loops, from which a key element eventually emerges.

You are perhaps wondering why homely business models like Gottlieb Duttweiler's Swiss grocery chain Migros, our own Tea Campaign, or Holger Johnson's ebuero have enjoyed such resounding success? Ultimately they are all typical of simple but well-thought out concepts.

In the case of the entrepreneurial concept for Ikea or Aldi, you could also ask yourself, "Why didn't I think of that?" But if we look closer, we see that very fundamental considerations stand behind these deceptively simple ideas.

Can you imagine furniture that the customer has to assemble himself? Can you design furniture that can be assembled without woodworking machinery or specialized tools? Doesn't this require a complete rethinking of how to make wardrobes, tables and chairs? Are customers even willing to put furniture together themselves? Do they have the time and inclination to do so? Do they dare? Isn't it unreasonable that people suddenly be required to assemble their own furniture? These are among the many novel questions that scarcely anyone before Ikea founder Ingvar Kamprad had ever asked . Did he get spontaneous positive feedback on these concerns from his circle of friends and acquaintances? I'm sure he didn't. The solution looks simple, but it demanded unconventional questions and a lot of mental effort before answers emerged: yes, customers were willing and able to assemble their furniture and, yes, the price incentives were sufficient to induce them to purchase furniture like this. Kamprad asked questions that, if they had even been asked previously, had elicited only negative responses. Kamprad had to challenge common sense and prevailing views, and he had no industry experts standing at his side. He had to rethink his furniture completely in order to figure out how to construct it so that ordinary consumers would be able to put it together at home.

Thus it's not a matter of inspiration or flashes of genius; it's about hard mental work. As long as you believe you have to wait for brilliant ideas, you won't get anywhere. Copernicus figured out that the earth revolved around the sun. The idea is really quite simple, isn't it? But to gain this insight required painstaking calculations and a change in very fundamental beliefs, which also proved to be highly dangerous for the astronomer Galileo who promoted this theory by Copernicus.

A few words about the 1950s. By then people in Germany were buying nice furniture again, replacing the makeshift solutions of the post-war period. Why would stores forego the aesthetic appointments that, the advertising people say, are needed to appeal to our emotions? Doing without such refinement was not a self-evident idea when the Albrecht brothers in Essen opened their first Spartan-looking stores, without all the store fixtures that had been customary up to then. It went counter to the views prevailing at the time, and no one would have believed that this would become the most successful grocery chain in Germany.

What can we learn from these two stories? Most people associate the word "idea" with inspiration. But this isn't what it's about. Apparently one can approach the development of an idea systematically and bring it to a successful conclusion. The magic formula is: "function, not convention." Use function as the starting point; do not follow conventions, however established.

Duttweiler demonstrated this for us. He sat in the City of Zürich's Statistical Office and combed through thousands of statistics, compared retail prices with those of other cities, calculated them backwards and forwards, and mapped out a concept that reads like a detective story in numbers. The title? "How Zürich Grocery Retailers Managed to Make the City the Most Expensive Area in Switzerland While at the Same Time Keeping the Citizens Indifferent."

Duttweiler, with some friends, founded the Migros Company in 1925. On August 25, early in the morning, five trucks rolled off to deliver their goods to the people. The trucks were loaded with only six products – coffee, rice, sugar, noodles, coconut oil, and soap. All in large packages. A flyer explained why these goods were so inexpensive, despite their high quality. The trucks and their drivers were a kind of consumer education on wheels. Duttweiler, the diligent researcher and discoverer of the obvious, proved to be a successful entrepreneur of the first order with his breakthrough as price cutter.[12]

Duttweiler can also be regarded as a pioneer in matters of efficiency. The Migros trucks were designed so that goods could be loaded into one side of the truck and conveniently unloaded from the other. Goods could be sold in odd quantities so that all prices could be in round numbers, which greatly facilitated making change. And prices were calculated to show the cost per 100-gram unit, creating price transparency despite the large and odd-sized packages. Those are little strokes of genius around the edges, but they show that Duttweiler thought in terms of a new simplicity. The world is becoming more complex every day, and we would have been overwhelmed long ago if occasionally someone hadn't appeared to make things simpler. Above all, Duttweiler thought systematically, and from that developed a concept that revolutionized the Swiss retail trade.

When people think of creativity, most think of brainstorming or sudden inspirations. Time and again I have found that good ideas are not spontaneous inspirations, but rather the result of systematic deliberation. Louis Pasteur knew that "fortune favors the prepared mind." When you have thought about a problem systematically, it can happen that the brilliant idea finally comes to you when you're taking a walk, playing tennis or just daydreaming. Creative minds and methods are stimulated and promoted by an *enriched environment*, that is, by a context rich in stimuli. Everyone needs a certain latitude and time-out during which you are not pursuing any narrowly focused goal-oriented activities.[13]

Karl Vesper, an American professor who researched more than 100 successful startups, also came to the conclusion that one can work *systematically* on the development of an idea and that this method makes an essential contribution to the success of a new business.

> One can approach the development of an idea totally purposefully and systematically.
>
> KARL VESPER

Below, we describe what we call the intelligent path to success. The only thing you need is a brain for thinking, and a certain tenacity.

However, I can guarantee that you will not be the first to go this route. By now, there has been an impressive number of startups of this kind. This book will report on a few of them. Take these people and companies as an inspiration and as role models. And recognize that startups can be very diverse – and a lot of fun. You could even say that starting a business is like starting a new love affair.

4.2 Developing your own concept

Your new love affair will begin completely risk-free. You don't need to invest anything and there will be no lean times to get through, nor long periods of work to put behind you. Start with an idea that you have had for a long time. What irritates me about some products? "Irritation is a great source of energy," according to Anita Roddick.

What do my friends and I lack? Couldn't we make certain things simpler, better, cheaper? What would I like to do, in collaboration with others? It's a question of finding an initial idea, selecting one from among the subjects you've already thought about.

Anyone who is actively creative – no matter what the field – knows that often the best ideas arise in moments of solitude, especially when the task is to work on a new puzzle rather than on an existing one. There is another situation that may help illustrate this principle: a school child who reads a classmate's essay is already caught in the web of that essay's thoughts.

Often original ideas arise only when you are working with a blank slate. Thus totally new ideas are not likely to be born when you put three experienced engineers together for three hours. While it's true that they will have a wealth of ideas, they will operate within, perhaps even be ensnared by, their own knowledge and the conventions that give meaning to their situation. Innovation is more likely to arise where established practices are challenged radically.

Now you're thinking: good; what I need is something radically different. Doesn't that mean that I need an invention of my own? No, you don't. Coming up with an invention and starting a business are not the same thing.

4.3 The difference between invention and innovation

Invention and innovation appear to be closely related. Many people believe there must be an invention at the beginning of every entrepreneurial success story. "The rest" is then merely a question of "implementation." This approach may seem plausible, but it's highly dangerous. In the history of new business ventures, there have probably been more failures of promising but immature ideas than there have been successful startups.

I know of no historical tale that illustrates the difference between invention and innovation more clearly than that of Charles Goodyear.[14] He hears about the properties of rubber, is fascinated and starts to work with this material. He has no money; to the contrary, he's had to flee from his creditors (much easier in his day than in ours). The year is 1833, and we're in Roxbury, Massachusetts. As promising as natural rubber appeared to be at first, and as infinite as the possibilities for using this material seem to be, it proves to be very difficult for Goodyear to manufacture usable products from it. Some of the material always remains soft and gummy, especially when it's hot. But in winter, when it gets very cold, it becomes brittle and hard as stone.

Goodyear begins to try out all sorts of substances, adding them to the natural rubber and conducting experiments. His family suffers. The three children get scarcely anything to eat. His wife lives with them outside of town and doesn't even have the money to visit her husband. By chance he comes upon a tip that sulfur is a good substance to improve the properties of natural rubber. Later he tries lead oxide. Once again, through luck and by chance something happens that will give rise to many legends in the history of research. By accident, a piece of rubber falls on the hot stove – and lo and behold, the heat transforms the material. Later Goodyear goes down in history as the man who invented the vulcanization of natural rubber.

In spite of this the company is not very successful. Goodyear's first promising order, 150 bags for the US Post Office, raises his hopes for revenue, but it turns out that the material doesn't have the properties required for the bags. One setback comes after another. One of the children falls ill. Goodyear can't afford a doctor, and the child dies. There's no money for a funeral either. His son is buried, and according to the neighbors, it's the most pitiful burial they've ever seen.

After many years his experiments show some success, and with the help of investor financing he's able to build a small factory. But fate strikes again. An unscrupulous businessman gets hold of Goodyear's knowledge: an angry shoemaker to whom Goodyear owes money reveals most of the manufacturing secrets. Because of the imitator, business is poor, and finally it becomes necessary to bring legal action – which Goodyear wins. Now you're thinking: here comes the happy end. He'll make money for the first time and the infringing competitor will have to pay the patent royalties retroactively. But then Goodyear falls gravely ill. His many years of working with lead oxide have taken their toll. He dies.

Where's the happy end? After all, we all know that there's a big company by the name of "Goodyear." How come this company isn't part of the story? Very simple. It has nothing to do with Goodyear – at least not with him as the founder. Many years later, two German immigrants made use of his knowledge and started a company with his name, in memory of him.

The story of Charles Goodyear is not an isolated case. The number of inventors who never managed to implement practical applications because some detail or other was overlooked, or whose invention was successfully implemented by someone else, is legion. The economist Schumpeter has drawn a crucial distinction from this: invention and innovation are two fundamentally different processes. According to Schumpeter, when we speak of establishing a business, it is the innovator, not the inventor, who plays the leading role.

4.4 The difference between entrepreneurship and business administration

At this point, it will be helpful to take another look at the relationship between the terms *entrepreneurship* and *business administration*. While the latter describes the organizational and administrative aspects of business, I propose that we use the term "entrepreneurship" to highlight the creative, innovative components of establishing a new business.

To conceptualize new things, it is necessary to have new tools, new language. The prospect of opportunities that will result from economic changes should not be sabotaged by the past. Accordingly we need new terminology. This isn't a question of merely redefining the terms, but rather showing that we are able to look at the entire field from a completely different perspective and gain new insights through more precise terminology.

There is no German word for entrepreneurship.[15] The term "*Unternehmer*" often translated as "businessman," "industrialist" or "contractor," embraces three very different functions:

1. the ownership function (who owns the company);
2. the management function (how the company is run from a business perspective);
3. the innovation function (the concept upon which the company is founded and further developed).

It is important to differentiate clearly between them because these tasks are very different and in the modern world can be addressed from a division-of-labor approach.

Let us stay with "entrepreneurship" and direct our focus to the creative components that drive an innovative startup. Which idea, which concept enables me, as a newcomer, to challenge established competitors?

The advice usually given to people starting businesses[16] still emphasizes mastery of business administration. But where is the founder's concept for the enterprise? It is mentioned only marginally. The prevailing view is that the founder brings the idea. "You want to have your own restaurant? Have you really thought it over, with all the competition that's out there?" "Good – now you have to address the business administration aspects: management, administration, financing, marketing, and much more." The idea itself is more or less regarded as a given. The crucial step, we are told, is to acquire the necessary business administration expertise in order to implement the idea with realistic performance targets.[17]

"What is an idea worth anyway?" Perhaps this is to some extent determined by the connotations of the word "idea." It sounds like an initial thought, something fleeting, theoretically detached and maybe somewhat idealistic. That an individual's own carefully thought-out idea could be the decisive factor for the success of a new business is not taken seriously in this literature.

However, it is possible to find literature that is more open-minded in this respect. If you take Timmons's model,[18] then the factors for success can be summed up in three groups: people, ideas and resources. Here at least a place has been made for a well-thought-out, well-developed idea. But even this approach places the emphasis on the organization of resources and on the business administration expertise of the founders and the management.

Only after the spectacular failures of numerous startups of the New Economy does it appear that people have begun to rethink this approach. Many of the startups between the years 1995 and 2000 drew upon the best management talent in the USA and enjoyed generous financing. Thus those factors could not be the grounds for their failure. No one will dispute that the Internet offers outstanding entrepreneurial opportunities. Private investors readily accept risk. Why then the high proportion of failures?

There was a lack of well-conceived and fully developed entrepreneurial concepts. A technology by itself does not provide an adequate concept for starting a business, and where such a concept is lacking, capital and management cannot make up for its absence. This is the lesson from the first Internet boom.

4.5 Patents and new technologies are only the raw material

Let's take these thoughts a little further. Until now we have tacitly assumed that startups originating from innovative concepts are neglected or overlooked by mainstream researchers and consultants, whose primary focus of attention has been on the so-called *technology-oriented* startups. An invention, the patent based on it, or a new technology, seemed to be a solid basis for establishing a new company.

But is this really true? Is a patent or new technology really a sufficient foundation for a new company, an invention that merely requires commercial implementation? Of course it is natural to demand that the many patents developed at universities and research facilities be implemented in entrepreneurial initiatives. As reasonable as such a demand may appear to be, based on the fact that so much money and work have been poured into the development of these patents, the critical issue has been overlooked. *What is decisive isn't the quality of an invention or technology, but rather its acceptance in the market.* The inventor or researcher may have achieved an exceptional breakthrough. He or she may even have received a Nobel Prize for it – but the economic success of a product is determined by the buyers, not the Nobel Committee. Research follows a different logic than the marketplace.

The essential link between an invention, research finding or a new technology on the one hand, and economic success in the marketplace on the other, is the entrepreneurial concept. This is the critical nexus between research orientation and market orientation. We will refer to this as *entrepreneurial design.*[19]

Importantly, entrepreneurial design is *not* commercial implementation. What is required in entrepreneurial design is an instinct for societal changes, a sensitivity to market developments. What you need are "truffle pigs," that is, a good nose plus intuition. Patents and new technologies are the raw

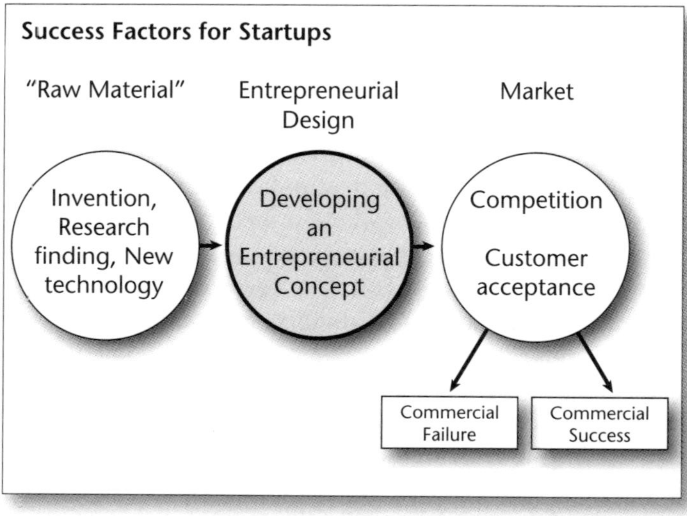

materials, but recognizing how they fit into an *entrepreneurial design* requires precisely those competencies that the economist Schumpeter identified in his model of the innovative entrepreneur.

Consequently it will not suffice just to give the inventor or researcher her own business consultant or MBA, who is then supposed to "transfer" the patent or new technology into practice. It is not self-evident that a line manager in a business really can master this task, even – and especially – if he is an illustrious "master" of business administration. Here we are not asking whether the current content of a business administration curriculum is tailored to the task of fostering an "instinct for future developments," whether a businessperson's ability to weigh risks can be learned through mathematical formulas, or whether this can be learned at all in an academic context. We are dealing with a different issue.

In the past the inventor-plus-business administrator model functioned well. The markets of the nineteenth and twentieth centuries concentrated on production. To be sure, sales didn't happen on their own, but they were not the main issue. Economists speak of a supply-oriented market when supply is the main focus of attention. Management and financing stood in the foreground. The brilliant engineer and the equally talented administrator together created a successful new company. The huge amounts of capital needed for the construction of steel plants, shipyards or textile factories made it necessary to procure the needed capital and to devote a great deal of attention to the financing needed to set up the business, and to accounting after it had been set up.

Today the bottleneck is no longer production but demand. There are more producers worldwide than ever before, and in many sectors there is surplus capacity. Competition is keen, and demand determines the market; economists refer to this as a demand-oriented market. Under these market conditions the critical task is to correctly assess the psychology of the markets and their changes, and to develop concepts that will survive in such a challenging environment.

This is something different from the competencies that constitute the instructional core of the training for a "Master of Business Administration" degree. The very term "administration" reveals from the outset that this training involves direction, but from a commercial-administrative perspective. Business Administration originated in order to maintain the oversight needed in large-scale businesses. This is where its strengths lie, not in working out innovative concepts for establishing new enterprises. The inventor-plus-administrator team was a successful model in an era when totally different conditions prevailed.

This also explains the lack of efficiency of the so-called transfer offices at universities and research facilities. It's not about brokering or transmission tasks. It is the transfer itself that requires true entrepreneurial imgination! And this requires entrepreneurs, not bureaucrats.

According to a study published in 2006 by the *Institut der Deutschen Wirtschaft* [Cologne Institute for Economic Research], "In Germany there are very many good ideas that find their expression in inventions and patents. However, problems often arise in the realm of implementation."[20] This sort of statement, found in many publications, appears to be perfectly reasonable – but is actually very misleading.

One could just as well say, "Humans are of divine descent and noble disposition. *However, problems often arise in the realm of implementation.*" Most certainly there is a divine spark in human beings, most of whom also want to behave well. But everyday life with its conflicts and complications shows us quite a different picture. The divine and the noble aspirations are at best raw material. The critical issues come to the surface only during implementation, or more precisely, in the *conception* of the implementation. Which political system is most suitable? What system of education? Which legal system? What form of penal administration? The word "implementation" clouds the real issues and makes it appear as if the most important issues had already been resolved and required only one very simple step, namely, implementation.

Patents and inventions are raw materials. Whether and how one can make use of them, what will prove its worth in the everyday life of the market – all of this remains unanswered.

This doesn't mean that there are no inventions and research results that can be easily converted into marketable products. But this isn't the norm. Even brilliant inventions or research findings are not automatically marketable. Research logic and market logic are fundamentally different.

4.6 What good entrepreneurial design must accomplish

We have to make high demands on entrepreneurial design because it must provide solutions to a whole range of problems faced by startups.

What good entrepreneurial design must accomplish

1. Work out clear market advantages
2. Secure a head start over imitators
3. Protect against technological obsolescence
4. Protect against commercial obsolescence
5. Minimize financing costs
6. Include marketing as an integral component of the entrepreneurial design

The first and most important criterion is that the concept demonstrates market advantages over established competitors. Business administrators are familiar with the marketing concept of the "unique selling proposition," that is, the feature that makes a product or service stand out from its competitors in the marketplace. But there is more to it than that. The greater this market advantage is, the greater a startup's chances of success. Thus it pays to tinker with the architecture of your design until you can work out a *significant* market advantage. Let's take an example from the Tea Campaign – the low price. Naturally, the more obvious your advantage over your competition, the better. But the advantage must also be clearly *identifiable*. Every butcher maintains that his pork chops are the best and the most reasonably priced. This means the customer must be able to perceive the advantage you offer and be able to judge its scope. In the case of the Tea Campaign, this was the selection of a type of tea well known for its high quality.

If you are successful, one thing is guaranteed – there will be imitators, and they can be very dangerous. If they have established sales channels, lots of capital and generous advertising budgets, there is a great risk that they will overtake you. Would a patent protect you here? The modern answer is yes, but only for a short time. As soon as the competition recognizes that there's a new solution, they too will devise other methods. According to Mitchell and Coles, a technological innovation will give a company an advantage of only six to twelve months at most. An advantage in the concept will have a longer effect, especially if you continuously refine it further.[21]

Let's take a look at the 1998 Berlin-Brandenburg Business Competition. One of the first prizes was awarded to the "Cortologic" Team, which had developed a speech recognition module that won praise from the jurors. And they weren't alone. Financial backers also found the concept convincing and invested in the company. Was this company still in existence ten years later? The answer is "no." Was this a surprise? Likewise, "no." Research on improved speech recognition technology is underway all over the world. Under these circumstances it was no mean feat that the team from Berlin was at the forefront of these developments – even if only for a short time. For how long? Tomorrow or the day after, in Taiwan, Singapore, Silicon Valley or Munich, there could be a breakthrough – or even just some minimally improved technology. In fact, there is a high probability that this will happen. From this perspective, it is highly risky, even futile, to hope to remain permanently in the vanguard. You have to meet the challenge of rapid technological obsolescence. If you are operating in a well-established and highly networked international research context, this may be realistic, but what about the rest of us ordinary mortals?

Even if we manage to stay at the top technologically, that by itself is not enough for success. The company also has to hold its ground against economic obsolescence. If tomorrow some item is produced in China in a larger series, with better economies of scale, your company may be left in the dust.

Paradoxically, what follows from these considerations is that a startup's chances of survival increase if it does *not* place its bets on its own hi-tech developments, but instead remains open and flexible and always purchases the technologically best-developed or most economically advantageous solutions on the market.

Naturally there are successful technologically oriented startups, but to be fair, in light of the intense research and competition worldwide, it's necessary to stress the high risks that exist for startup entrepreneurs with a high-tech product.

The smaller the financing burden your entrepreneurial design requires, the better it is for you. Not only are you spared the humbling treks to banks and other financial backers, but you are better off overall. In particular, the less outside financing you need (that is, capital you will have to pay back, capital which will not be counted as an asset of your company), the less danger there is that you'll be forced into a liquidity squeeze because fearful bankers precipitously lose confidence in your prospects for success and call their loans. It pays to spend the time to puzzle out how to keep capital costs as low as possible. It's important that you make the size of capital expenditures a measure of the quality of your entrepreneurial design.

The same applies to marketing, a function that also belongs in your concept. We can formulate this as a principle: the more unusual the idea, the greater your chances of attracting the public's attention. In marketing, being a bit offbeat is a positive factor. What does your market advantage have to look like for your marketing to be easy? Above all, it's your concept that determines how successful your marketing can be. Marketing must go hand in hand with the development of your idea; it cannot be an afterthought, a mere add-on. Marketing is an integral component of a sound entrepreneurial concept. It should not be, "We've got a product – now how are we going to sell it?"

If we keep all these points in mind, it becomes clear how much more is involved in a concept than a mere inspiration or an incipient idea. Abraham Lincoln is said to have once declared, "If I had ten hours to chop down a tree, I would use the first eight to sharpen my ax." This should also be the approach for starting a company. In the realm of concept-creative startups, it is the quality of the entrepreneurial design that decides the success of a company.

Your entrepreneurial design will be truly excellent if you are able to adhere to three additional principles in working out the puzzle that is your idea.

Principles for a High-Potential Entrepreneurial Design

- Scalability
- Simplicity
- Minimization of Risk

The concept must permit scalability. The output must be replicable, if possible in such a way that if growth does occur, capacities will not have to be expanded proportionately, but synergy effects will kick in. Software is the best-known example for this. Professionally programmed software makes this possible. Even in the event of an unexpectedly large expansion, programs don't have to be rewritten. (Quite a contrast from the Tea Campaign's first years, when as we grew we had to start from scratch three times with totally new software.)

Simplicity is a helpful principle. Most of the errors associated with startups arise from complexities that have not been brought under control. In newly established companies problems multiply, especially when there is rapid growth leading to the typical growth crises. As the old saying goes, "Any idiot can make things complicated." It requires brains to think things through, to keep them as simple and manageable as possible.

> Complexity kills.
> It sucks your energy, flow and creativity.
>
> AUTHOR UNKNOWN

"Be ready to take a risk!" This is an often-heard, but nonetheless really foolish statement – at least when told to startup entrepreneurs. Instead, the principle should be, "As an entrepreneur, avoid risk as much as possible."

We can illustrate this through the example of a mountain climber. To climb a challenging mountain, you must not only prepare well, but you must also, as far as you can, eliminate all foreseeable risks. Enough risks will always remain, even for the experienced mountaineer. Precisely because you're moving in high-risk territory, you have to avoid as many risks as possible. A single misstep can mean death; the failure rate is high. Down in the lowlands, or as civil servants we may be more willing to tolerate risk, but as entrepreneurs we can't afford to.

"Many problems can be identified only in actual practice." Yes, that is a true statement. "The moment you have started, all hell breaks loose," noted the experienced start-up founder Guy Kawasaki. But the implication can only be that since hell breaking loose is to be expected and you knew about it in advance, you should be well prepared, having considered the foreseeable risks. Incidentally, Winston Churchill is a good advisor in such situations. His advice? "If you go through hell, keep going!"

Of course, theory and practice are very different. Imagine being asked to walk on a tightrope. To the left and the right, you are looking down into a void. Your coach tells you it's very easy. You only have to keep your balance. And he's right. At least in theory. He can even write the formula for balance on the blackboard. And the formula is right, too. But what good does that do you? Is it really about balance? When you walk across a rope that is only 10 cm above the ground, it's easy as pie. When the rope is stretched 20 meters above the ground, theoretically it is still a matter of balance. But practically there is a huge difference. Fear comes into play; childhood failures are re-awakened, and your ability to perform under stress plays a huge role.

You should look for role models or advisors who have walked that tightrope, and as many times as possible.

Let me re-emphasize: you need a very sound and fully developed concept. That takes time. This doesn't mean you should work slowly, or be overly hesitant. However, perfecting the concept under time pressure may not work well. And you may need to turn a deaf ear to friends or acquaintances: "You've talked about this for so long, why don't you finally just do it?" Keep working until you are ready.

4.7 Working at the Puzzle

Good entrepreneurial design is the result of a search process much like trying things out and piecing together a jigsaw puzzle. The process is similar to creating a composition where you keep working until everything fits and every false note has been eliminated.

But where do you get the faith that at the end of all this work you'll find a concept that will leave your competition in the dust? Haven't many others already tried? How can you, perhaps an outsider without years of experience, hope to find a winning solution? After all, you're a perfectly ordinary human being, without special evidence of genius or luck, aren't you?

I want to share a little story with you. I'm a student and I'm driving through southern France in my old VW. A hitchhiker is standing by the side of the road. I'm alone and I pick him up. We get into a conversation, and I ask him what kind of work he does. He says he's a disk jockey – in the Seychelles. Wow, I say, a DJ in the Seychelles – what a super job. The guy looks totally normal. How do you get a job like that? He says it wasn't particularly difficult. Not hard? I ask. There have to be ten thousand people dreaming of a job like that! How did he manage it? He says he looked up the addresses of hotels on the Seychelles, he drafted a letter, and one hotel wrote him to come out there. Sure, I say, but thousands of others must have done the same thing. No, he says: he was the only one!

Haven't you heard people say to you (and perhaps you are saying this to yourself!), "Don't think for a minute you're the first person with this idea!" Think about the Tea Campaign. Did I invent economy-sized packaging? Was I the one who discovered you could avoid the middlemen? No. But these two puny ideas, neither brilliant nor creative, applied to a field where no company had ever used them before, has made the Tea Campaign the biggest importer of Darjeeling tea in the world.

So look for a field of your own and start to analyze it. What principles could change the conditions in this field to your advantage? Don't let yourself be deterred by well-meaning friends and acquaintances who don't want to believe that you have found something that works.

But if you get to the point of giving up, take a tip from Daniel Goleman, an psychology professor who made a name for himself with his study of emotional intelligence. He describes the difference between a genius and an ordinary person. There is but one small difference, but it's decisive. Both persons work on a problem, and neither one can solve it. Both have to decide whether to give up because the problem seems intractable. But here is the difference. The ordinary person gives up, which seems reasonable, in light of the time wasted and the hopelessness of the task. The genius, according to Goleman, also gives up – but not entirely. He pushes the problem back into the recesses of his subconscious – and waits. And it so happens that a pattern turns up at a totally different place than the path where he had been looking for it. Because he didn't abandon the problem totally, he now has a chance to recognize the pattern and apply it to the problem on the back burner of his mind .[22]

Is there a guarantee that you'll find a solution to your problem? Not at all. How long should you stick it out? Persevere: after all, it doesn't cost you anything to keep a semi-conscious thought in the back of your mind and check on its progress from time to time.

I believe it's helpful to treat this mental activity as a form of recreation, just as you would work a real puzzle. After a little practice, it gets easier to move the pieces around to see if they fit. You should get just as much pleasure from this as a child who enjoys puzzles and takes satisfaction each time the pieces fit. It is a game or a sport. The Danish philosopher Søren Kierkegaard worked simultaneously at six separate desks because he found that when he was writing one text, ideas would come to him for the other texts he wasn't working on at that moment. You, too, can play at a number of puzzles at the same time.

4.8 Creating an idea that is a work of art

In Italy, the cradle of so much European art, there is the concept of *concetto* – the intellectual blueprint for a work yet to be created: the sketch or plan is referred to as the *disegno*. In German we have the concept of a *Gesamtkunstwerk*, a term used by Richard Wagner to express the idea that one can meld a variety of different arts into an artistic whole that is greater than the sum of its parts. The development of successful business concepts can also make use of these disparate elements. New approaches often come from people who stand outside a particular business sector or from newcomers to the market for whom the existing customs and usages have not yet become second nature, who can still question them critically.

Good entrepreneurial design is something that one might call *plain style*, where one has tightened, simplified and looked deeply into the substance of a work until one has eliminated every superfluous ornament. In economics, this means saving on manpower, capital, energy, materials, and transportation. Like good literature, good art or good music, good entrepreneurial design may draw its power from simplicity and clarity.

> Simplicity
> is the ultimate sophistication
>
> LEONARDO DA VINCI

"Simplicity, simplicity, simplicity!" urges Henry David Thoreau in his most famous book, *Walden*. The counterprinciple, complexity, requires much greater professional expertise and holds much greater risks. Thus a founder is well advised to keep his concept as simple as he possibly can: to endow things with a new simplicity that is economically compelling.

It is not knowledge or research findings that are traded in the marketplace, but rather products and services that embody a new physical or intellectual *gestalt*.[23] Thus we can also speak of *entrepreneurial gestalt*.

For designers a user-centered orientation is part of their profession; design is the link between object and user. This analogy transfers very well to our problem. A connection must be built from the invention, the research findings or the new technology to the user. Anyone who doesn't build this bridge may be pursuing a development that is interesting technologically, but he may drive right past the market.

The task of working up a good entrepreneurial design doesn't end with starting a company. Even a superlative entrepreneurial design doesn't mean that we can rest on our laurels. Market situations change and new technologies develop, which is why work on the entrepreneurial design is an on-going task.

Today, it is possible to have startups that are not defined by capital and technology but by the creativity and ideas of their founders, even if creative power and passion seldom go hand and hand with business administration.

These days an entrepreneur is more like an artist than a manager. The close relationship between entrepreneurship and artistic endeavor is sometimes even reflected in word choice. See how Steve Wozniak, the co-founder of Apple, describes his work:

> "A good engineer is like an artist. When you develop something, every detail is like a brushstroke that has to be exactly right.
> Just as Ernest Hemingway worked at polishing his sentences for days and weeks, I work at Apple.
> We composed like solo musicians.
> From notes come melodies, then stanzas and finally an entire song."
>
> STEVE WOZNIAK

In the 19th century, many artists came to be seen as revolutionary, as antitheses to the businessman and his bourgeois moral philosophy. With the changes in industrial capitalism and the shift away from its bureaucratic notions of organization, modern management philosophies are oriented to ideals like flexibility, creativity and innovation. And with this shift more and more points of contact arise between these two worlds. According to the French sociologist Pierre-Michel Menger, the artist becomes the prototype and ideal. If art was deemed the rather exotic alternative model to the subordinate and alienating world of dependent labor, as the realm of freedom in contrast to the realm of necessity, it has since developed into a model for creative living.[24] Entrepreneurship: the art of self-determination, the conqueror of conventions, the practice of creative destruction.[25]

4.9 Understand the principle and you can start many businesses

The best evidence that one can successfully and practically separate entrepreneurship from business administration is the existence of "serial entrepreneurs," that is, people who have established a whole array of businesses. While the "businessman = manager" has his hands full – and often too full – with the responsibilities of running only a single business, this species of multi-founders is able to lighten the heavy load through delegation.

Holger Johnson is just such a multi-founder. In addition to ebuero, he has established, co-founded or functioned as a business angel actively engaged in the development of about 20 other companies. How does he do it? He concentrates on the entrepreneurial design, from which he formulates objectives and tasks and then supervises their execution. In this way he uses his head and his time in the area in which he excels. He knows full well that he must not permit too much complexity in his entrepreneurial design work. A high degree of complexity would increase susceptibility to error and require more decision-making on his part; it would sap more of his energy and divert his attention from the areas where his best talents lie – and from what he most enjoys.

If you look at Richard Branson, another serial entrepreneur, you don't get the impression that he is overburdened with work. There is an air of originality about him; he seems to be having a lot of fun, and he pursues extravagant and expensive hobbies. Is he a total genius, a person who would always be successful, no matter what he tried? Don't jump to any conclusions: anyone who has read his autobiography gets a very different picture. The beginning was difficult. For a long time he didn't earn anything. He played cute with the customs authorities, got himself arrested and spent a night in jail, followed by a big fine. What made the difference was the persistence with which he worked on his ideas. He didn't allow himself to be trapped in the little world of the self-employed, the someone-who-has-to-do-everything, the jack-of-all-trades. The title of his book, "Business is like Rock 'n' Roll," doesn't sound like bookkeeping, accounting and monotony. We urgently need someone like Branson in the world of entrepreneurship to "*bransonize*" the startup scene.

Muhammad Yunus, winner of the Peace Nobel Prize, is a serial entrepreneur in the social sphere. The Grameen Bank with its microcredits is only one of the many enterprises he has promoted. They include the solar energy company Grameen Shakti, as well as Grameen Phone, already a telecommunications giant, and Grameen Danone, a joint venture for the production of fortified yogurt, designed to make up for nutritional deficiencies typical among Bangladesh's rural population. The Grameen group even includes an investment company. Yunus uses the tools of capitalism because he is convinced that it is possible to use our economic system more efficiently than it is being used today. Anyone who has ever had anything to do with him perceives him as relaxed, amiable, totally present and *not* overburdened, even if his multiplicity of projects and duties would lead you to expect that.

The fact that founders can be trained to develop successful entrepreneurial designs and conceive of their second business more easily than the first has been confirmed by empirical studies of serial entrepreneurs.[26] After the first startup you understand what it involves; once you get the hang of it, you can found multiple businesses. Each successive time Holger Johnson does it better, faster and with fewer financial resources. Just as you can learn to put a puzzle together faster and better, you get better at entrepreneurial design.

The principle is to develop ever more intelligent economic solutions, systematically and creatively, solutions that are profitable in the marketplace and create commercial assets both for the entrepreneur and for his customers. It's an enormously complex task that demands time and knowledge. And the required skills cannot be acquired through theory alone.

Anyone who arrives fresh on the market must be at least twice as good and half as expensive as the competition: that is Holger Johnson's motto. His ebuero even works with a 90% savings for the customer. A process like this requires intensive analysis of an idea, but this way you can get all kinds of startups with great potential, not just hi-tech startups. In my experience this type of high-*potential* startup has even greater prospects of success than a startup based on hi-tech alone. Moreover, its need for financing and exposure to risk may also be smaller.

The clearer and simpler the result, the more work is needed in advance. It usually requires thousands of building blocks of information before an idea reaches conceptual maturity. Often successful founders have spent years gestating an idea and have invested a prodigious amount of time and energy in this intellectual effort.[27]

It is important to work out the factors for success accurately, because so many startups fail. Depending upon which study you want to believe, the failure rate lies between 30 and 80 (!) percent.[28]

Anyone who doesn't have a competitive advantage will find it difficult to hold his own against companies already in the market. The competition already has a customer base and knows the distinctive features of the market; they have accumulated experience and financial reserves, and are also in a better position to assess the risks than a newcomer would be. In short, established competitors have advantages in all the important areas. So you have to come up with something special to make it in the marketplace: your innovative concept is the crucial factor. For us ordinary mortals it is the decisive trump card for a startup.

4.10 Successful companies originate in the mind

Developing a good entrepreneurial concept is a challenge, whether it is the result of arduous work or cheerful contemplation.[29] Many paths are traveled better in one's head than with one's feet. "Sometimes one needs as much as ten years and 50,000 pieces of information before an entrepreneurial concept is born," notes Professor Simon of Carnegie Mellon University. Simon's experience should not frighten us, but it demonstrates that a well-thought-out idea is not a trivial and fleeting thing that gains substance only after it has been implemented through "business administration."

This development is a process during which problems, possible solutions, alternatives and risks are sorted, sifted and weighed until a balanced and well-proportioned concept emerges, which can withstand the buffetings of the marketplace. This is not a fast process. "Today the fast devour the slow" is a fashionable mantra – but "faster" can also mean faster into bankruptcy. Letting an idea ripen does not mean wasting time. In the highly competitive hi-tech sector, time is indeed a critical factor, but this is not automatically true for all other areas of entrepreneurship. The "discovery of slowness" has also achieved good and lasting results, *e.g.* with "slow food."

It is helpful, even at the very start, to anticipate many of the typical scenarios that will emerge later, such as the problem of imitators, and to have solutions ready. Not because it is really possible to foretell market behavior, but because improvisation and planning complement each other.[30] Most often, good planning is the prerequisite for good improvisation.

May I mention that good entrepreneurial design also includes personal life goals?

My students are usually amazed when I ask successful founders about the number of hours they spend working; these founders reply that there is relatively little work for them to do in their ongoing businesses – provided that there was a really good concept to start with. In fact, empirical studies acknowledge that there are successful businesses not associated with intensive work. Thus the phenomenon already exists – but it has been overlooked, or downplayed because it didn't fit in with preconceived notions.[31]

Like a patent, entrepreneurial design has intrinsic value, as shown by Ingvar Kamprad's Ikea concept and the Aldi brothers' model. When the word "patent" is used here, it is not in the sense of a protectable right, but rather as a thought process that has resulted in something new in which there is inherent value. Perhaps there will come a day when we will grant the same rights to entrepreneurial concepts that are currently awarded to patentable concepts in the engineering and scientific disciplines.

Successful companies originate in the mind. The better an entrepreneurial concept is and the more it is analyzed and fine-tuned, the more it will resemble a finished work of art and the more likely it is to be successful.

Architecture provides another example. Leading architects have always sought to create structures that fit in with the place, the era and available materials, most often under the constraint of limited resources. Thus the task begins with the search for a structural concept. Before construction begins, the building originates as a plan in the mind of the architect, who positions and repositions individual features, weighs options, makes selections and perhaps starts afresh, and works on the missing pieces of the puzzle until the separate pieces fit together. Of course it is true that many problems will emerge only during construction. However, it would be disastrous to conclude from this that construction should be commenced before the architect had worked out the structural concept and formulated a technically feasible plan. Good architecture expresses a sense of perfection. It is not without reason that architecture is not considered just a technical profession but is also admitted to have a creative, artistic component. It should be added that architect and builder represent two different functions – like the entrepreneur and manager; it is not expected that the architect erects the building himself.

The modern entrepreneur isn't the genius who must combine in his own person the abilities of a strategic commander, a scientist and a PR man. Even small ideas can have a big impact as long as they are good ideas. The field of economics is *not* an area in which all ideas have already been imagined and realized. It is a field that is *lacking* in ideas, a field much in need of improvement, from everyday products to major issues like transportation, environment and health.

Small is Beautiful was a famous book title from the 1960s, but its subtitle was even better – *Economics as if People Mattered*. We need an economy where people play the decisive role: one that places the advancement of mankind at its center. Economics as a discourse needs more precision, more *nuance*: a higher development, a refinement, a sophistication of the system.

Just as we have refined our taste buds on our journey from caveman to *haute cuisine*, so have our needs in the other areas of our lives become more highly developed and more demanding. We know that good cooks need more than bare cooking skills. They need imagination, a love of experimentation, the ability to recognize trends and to react to a new range of problems (the dream of an earthly paradise has given way to the dream of a slender figure). And last but not least, pleasure and satisfaction in the work itself are important prerequisites for success.

The economy I envision could be an economy in which the crucial impulses come from entrepreneurs who contribute economic, social and, yes, artistic imagination, using modern, efficient means to create value.

John Ruskin and William Morris, the founders of the Arts and Crafts Movement in England, recognized the dehumanizing trends of the Industrial Revolution. They urged that the achievements of technology and economics be used in the interest of higher-quality and more aesthetic products.

This isn't a matter of a quest for paradise or utopia. It is much simpler – it is about fewer bad products that harm our pocketbooks or our health. Or fewer products with a short life span.

Thomas Hoof, the founder of the German company Manufactum, is also fighting for more quality. He points out that today the enemy of the good isn't the better, but the worse, the cheaper, the banal: there is scarcely a quality product that isn't jeopardized by pathetically poor but much cheaper competitors and knock-offs.[32]

"A thing ... should serve its purpose perfectly; that is, fulfill its function practically, be durable, cheap and attractive." This quotation from Walter Gropius (1925) from the early Dessau years of the Bauhaus can continue to be our guide today. By pointing to more simplicity, it also offers us the luxury of reduced complexity. Architecture still has much to teach us about the relationship of form and function.[33]

5 Avoiding Overload

5.1 The entrepreneur as Jack-of-all-trades – and why we have to get rid of this old saw

So you want to start a company? What is crucial for this to succeed? Most start-up consultants are unanimous in their answer to this question: first and foremost, you should have good business administration skills! Getting this expertise and applying it correctly is critical! The better trained a founder is in areas like management, marketing or finance, the greater his chance of success!

Sound convincing? It's actually terrible advice.

What founders supposedly need:
Areas of expertise traditionally required

- ✔ Bookkeeping
- ✔ Accounting
- ✔ Controlling

- ✔ Industry experience
- ✔ Labor, corporate and tax law
- ✔ Negotiating skills

- ✔ Management and organization
- ✔ Personnel management
- ✔ Inventory management

- ✔ Marketing and sales
- ✔ Customer communications
- ✔ Finance
- ✔ Public relations

The recommendation is that a founder should be a jack-of-all-trades. Not only does he have to be well-versed in accounting, but he also has to be familiar with finance, management, marketing, labor law, contract and tax law. He must be able to negotiate with banks, customers and suppliers. He should provide his staff with leadership and handle public relations adroitly. He must have a firm grasp of balance sheets and controlling.

Yes, here he is again, our extreme-sport personality with masochistic tendencies. He's supposed to be able to handle all of that – and his marathon gets longer every day. Although this catalog is impressive enough as it is, you have to keep in mind that these are only the general headings for entire fields of expertise; in some cases the required expertise is broken down into so many subfields that a single individual could scarcely cover all the bases (take labor law or tax law, for example). These are areas for which you need months or years of solid training to be able to perform with sufficient competence.

In addition, these subject areas are constantly expanding in breadth and depth, so what might have been realistic in the past, i.e. to perform more or less competently in these fields, is no longer feasible. In this situation there is no other solution than to compensate somehow for one's personal lack of expertise.

So before we urge all you non-economists to familiarize yourselves with this mass of material – as conventional start-up consultants would do –, we should stop and think for a moment. The following statement was made by the founder of Body Shop:

> If I had gone to business school,
> I never would have started the company.
>
> ANITA RODDICK

We suspect that not only Ms. Roddick, but many other potential founders as well are deterred by the prospect of having to train themselves in all those diverse business fields. But not every one has Anita Roddick's courage to simply leap over this hurdle.

But this catalog of job requirements which, after all, is not off the mark, does not need to be fulfilled by a single person. Only a genius could meet all those requirements, but mere mortals would inevitably fail. What management theoretician Fredmund Malik says about executives can also be applied to entrepreneurs.[34]

You can describe the ideal type, but you won't find him in the real world. So you have to pose the question differently. "How can we enable ordinary people – because ultimately we'll never have enough talent – to deliver exceptional results?"[35]

And another objection: those fields are so large and so challenging that you'd be in danger of ending up as a dilettante, and dilettantism is even more dangerous than admitting you have not mastered the field.

And the list above isn't even complete. Totally absent are the crucial competencies that *founders* need in order to be able to hold their own in the market. Founders must recognize new trends and sense market changes in a timely manner, while continually adapting their business concept to match new market conditions. They must make their ideas plausible and convincing and kindle their employees' enthusiasm. They must *lead* their companies.[36] This is quite different from organizing and managing the day-to-day aspects of a business,[37] which already includes more than enough tasks to fill a single individual's workday.

Modern companies are based on a division of labor, and this didn't just start yesterday. The moral philosopher Adam Smith recognized the increasing division of labor as a condition for national prosperity, or "the wealth of nations," as he put it. The first factory based on the division of labor was a shoe factory located in the kingdom of Philip II of Macedonia, from which Philip's son, Alexander the Great, is said to have drawn the inspiration for his art of war. Why, then, do we continue to demand that a founder be proficient in all conceivable management, social and legal functions?

A modern entrepreneur needs to be able

- ✔ To develop an innovative concept of his own
- ✔ To implement his concept
- ✔ To continue to develop his concept
- ✔ To adapt his concept to changing conditions
- ✔ To inspire his employees with enthusiasm for his concept
- ✔ To monitor the market
- ✔ To recognize new trends and technological developments early on
- ✔ To prepare and make decisions on direction
- ✔ To be the authority for all fundamental decisions

5.2 Recognize your own ignorance, or: the art of judgment and cooperation

You ask, and rightly so, how you can delegate a task that you yourself are not acquainted with. How can I place bookkeeping in someone else's hands and still control it? How can I delegate something and demand quality if I haven't mastered the subject myself? Won't I be taken in by charlatans, by swindlers and crooks? Won't the control of my own company be wrested from my hands? Or will the company sail into straits I wish to avoid? Will I be able to stay on top of things, or will I get into situations I can't master?

There are, of course, a thousand good reasons why such competencies are important, so it seems thoroughly justified and plausible when conventional wisdom tells us that becoming well-versed in business management areas is indispensible. But is this an insurmountable problem? Not at all.

The objection:

How can I judge qualifications
when I myself don't have
the relevant experience?

Let's stop for a moment and examine our daily lives. There are many other areas of life where knowledge and specialization have increased to such a degree that it is no longer possible to become fully competent in a multiplicity of areas. Do we recognize any analogies to this problem? What could we borrow by way of analogy from other areas of our lives?

Imagine you go to the doctor. Naturally you want a skilled diagnostician. How do you assess the quality of a doctor? It's obvious, isn't it? You have to study medicine. But please, not just the first four semesters – or you'll be convinced that you yourself have every disease in the book. Now imagine you go to a lawyer. How are you supposed to judge his competence? Law school is a must. Your next appointment takes you to the dentist, an auto mechanic or an architect. How are you going to assess their qualifications? All of these are daily occurrences in every modern society. You've been making these judgments without prior relevant experience for a long time without even noticing. How did you manage?

You ask friends and colleagues, you refer to the relevant literature, you google it on the Internet. Or you create your own impressions, evaluate the reactions of the parties involved, and so forth. Can you transfer these observations to our problem? I think you can. In the same way that we are already working with a variety of specialized professionals in our own daily lives, we have to imagine the entrepreneur functioning in the future.

> You don't have to be an ox
> in order to judge beef.
>
> KARL KRAUS
> Literary Critic

To delegate effectively, it is important to find partners who understand your undertaking, share your enthusiasm for it, and also have the required expertise – demonstrated by the fact that they can present their specialized knowledge in a way that can be generally understood. (Except perhaps in Germany, scarcely anyone is deemed knowledgeable if he cannot express himself clearly.) You know from your own experience that it is important to cooperate with your attorney and that being in the right, by itself, is not enough. Your attorney instructs you that you must collect evidence and that you must be objective. And you would do well to follow his advice.

You must delegate to qualified people (not necessarily your own employees), and you can do this just as you do in other aspects of your life. To Enzo Ferrari, the motor sport legend, is attributed the following statement:

> I've never understood much about engines.
> I have my engineers for this.
>
> ENZO FERRARI

You can perform outstandingly even in an area where you don't understand the details.

At the beginning of this third millennium of the modern era, we are confronted every day with situations in which we must act quickly and knowledgeably even though we are not trained in a particular area of expertise. Strangely, this idea has not yet been accepted in the realm of entrepreneurship.

But why shouldn't this principle apply especially to entrepreneurship? The model of a businessman as a multi-talented jack-of-all-trades is passé. The modern division of labor, along with virtuality, provides innovative start-ups with a new contextual framework. Today the founders of a company or their team don't need to do everything themselves. They only need to know where they can get reliable information, how to inform themselves sufficiently to assess its quality, and how to evaluate advice objectively. Good, old-fashioned common sense and instinct often help more than expertise in all sorts of specialties.

You will surely accrue knowledge and develop expertise in individual areas in the course of working in your company. Our point is only that too much is demanded of you as a *founder* if you have to develop expertise in all these necessary subjects.

Google is a good example of how a company can develop a superior concept and prevail against established search engines. The two founders, Sergey Brin and Larry Page, concentrated on the search for the best search results that would combine customer wishes with market logic. Google is not managed by its founders, but by the experienced professional manager Eric Schmidt – an example of a successful division of labor between entrepreneurship and business administration.

Doesn't leadership require a certain distance from the daily grind, a bit of downtime? How are you supposed to keep your eye on the horizon and identify new developments quickly if you are totally wrapped up in the organization?

The difference between business administration and entrepreneurship is extremely important because these terms delineate two different fields of activity. At issue is not whether one can separate the two fields for practical organizational reasons, but rather that each field imposes a different set of requirements. In its essence entrepreneurship is a creative act. According to Timmons, it is the ability to create something out of practically nothing.[38] Thus entrepreneurship demands a creative, visionary mindset, while business administration requires organizing, controlling and administrative abilities.[39]

Because most people do not possess both kinds of abilities, it is asking too much of founders to perform both kinds of activities. Instead, a division of labor will enable the founders to turn to the creative aspects of the business.[40] As a founder, then, you must work *on* your business, but not necessarily *in* your business. The notion that founders must be able to do everything is a relic from the last century – actually the century before last. It is high time to give it up.

5.3 Where startup consultants fail: the example of Dorothee the artist

Dorothee is the daughter of a colleague of mine. She was an English major but didn't want to become a teacher. In her free time she creates vases, large ceramic pieces. She asked me whether she couldn't make a little business out of this. I asked her a whole series of questions. Did she really enjoy doing it? Did she enjoy it so much that she could imagine doing it over the long term? Are people willing to buy these vases with their own money? And much more. Dorothee explained that she really did enjoy working on her ceramics. That there are people who are buying her vases already and that she is earning money with them, even when she calculates all her expenses and her own work time. And that if she wanted to, she could ask for more money.

This didn't sound bad. In fact, it sounded very convincing. Dorothee would probably be happier with her vases than she would be working as a teacher in a job she disliked. My advice: do it. Don't let yourself be dissuaded; bet on your artistic talent.

I ran into her again a few months later. Curious, I ask her about her business. "I'm not suited to be a business person," she tells me. "How so?" I ask, amazed. Dorothee explains that she took a course in starting a business, but – "I failed the balance sheet analysis."

Balance sheet analysis is something valuable. Nobody who wants to understand the financial situation of a major company like Siemens can skip the balance sheet analysis. But what Dorothee needed isn't a balance sheet analysis. What she needs to know is whether her work is generating enough income. Every street kid in Manila, every woman in Bangladesh who gets a microcredit from the Grameen Bank, has the business smarts for this, without formal business administration concepts and techniques. A formal requirement just frightens people off, especially creative, artistically inclined people. The start-up consultant would have given better advice if he had simple told Dorothee to collect the receipts for her expenses and her income and take them to a bookkeeper, or to pay a student to do her income tax return. With Dorothee, a promising business founder was derailed because of an incompetent startup consultant.

5.4 "A business of your own means the business owns you"

A business founder cannot and must not be able to do everything. At least not these days.

It is instructive to examine the situation of many small business owners from this perspective. They start a restaurant, a beauty salon, a clothing boutique or a copy shop, and then they nearly work themselves to death. As imitative startups without clearly identifiable market advantages, businesses like this lose out to the competition because they have little or nothing of their own to compete with. Instead of leading (and that means identifying market developments early on and improving their products), they get worn down in the minutiae of the day-to-day business. They didn't develop a concept of their own, but instead simply started a business and now they can barely keep their heads above water. Unfortunately, the witticism that "a business of your own means the business owns you" is all too applicable to their situation. As a rule, those students of mine whose parents are self-employed are the ones who most resist the idea of starting a business. The images they grew up with, the burdens and the risks, the stress of keeping up with bills, the problems with employees, the complaints about high taxes, the anxiety about the next inventory, are all too familiar to them and scare them off.

It makes a big difference whether or not you are doing something that you chose yourself, according to your own inclinations. This is especially true for entrepreneurship. One kind of entrepreneur is like a surfer, filled with enthusiasm for the sport, and with optimism in the face of a challenge. For him, it is a pleasure to be in the wind and the waves, which are taken as positive challenges. If something goes wrong, the surfer gets back on his surfboard as quickly as he can and keeps going. He learns from his mistakes and does not experience setbacks as defeats. He is receptive to learning and builds on his inclinations and talents. He naturally reaches out for all the knowledge and innovations he can grasp, and reworks them in a creative and efficient way.

Now let us imagine someone who, whether by fate or because there was an unfilled niche in the market, is doing work that is *not* in line with his inclinations and talents. He is more like a person on a sailing ship in heavy seas who can't do anything at all with the waves and the water. He feels that all the elements have conspired against him, and he curses the waves and the wind. Not only is he in a difficult situation, but he is in a desperate mood too. He only sees the storm and wishes he were somewhere else. He is not very receptive to ideas on improving the sail, the rudder, or his skills.

The same set of facts may be perceived very differently by two different individuals, and their reactions as well as their willingness to learn from their experience may be diametrically opposite. It's not difficult for us to foresee the results of their actions.

Of course, not all people are fortunate enough to be able to follow their own inclinations and talents. What we are saying here is only this: as a founder, you must take into account your own personality, your own inclinations, your strengths and weaknesses. A sense of duty and work ethic alone will rarely give you the high energy required to found a business. The idea and the field of activity must fit the founder.

Against this background, you will understand why you won't read much about the concept of market niches in this book. The advice that founders look out for a niche in the market is short-sighted. If there are only three copy shops located in my neighborhood and if the number of residents and their level of income would support a fourth copy shop, should I start one? The market-niche view says yes, this is a good opportunity. To some entrepreneurship theoreticians, nothing is more important than the concept of "opportunity recognition." My advice is: "Don't do it!" Recognizing opportunities is not the same as working out a concept. You should not spend your working life doing something that you don't enjoy, something that deadens your spirit. Holger Johnson says, "I hate opportunities; they are dangerous." They distract us from well-thought-out plans, without opening up long-term prospects. Opportunities are ephemeral phenomena. Starting a business may well be the road to your own bondage. Finding an idea and developing it is different from looking for opportunities and niches in the market.

Yet another problem crops up if you take on all those management tasks. It is never easy to become the boss and lead with authority the very people with whom you've been interacting on an equal, collegial level. For this reason, some founders don't want to lead because they long for the friendly camaraderie of the past. But most *cannot* lead because they are already overwhelmed by trying just to organize and discipline themselves. With my students I have observed time and again that if the founding team has previously worked together, they are fairly able to cope with this. If, however, additional staff are hired – who as a rule are less motivated and not accustomed to the informal working style of the founders –, clearer instructions are needed, and the founder must have the will and ability to stick to the founding concept, especially an innovative concept that may not be self-evident or make sense to everyone.

This is a classic problem when you hire staff coming fresh from the university, where it is axiomatic to question and discuss everything. In a start-up, however, what is critical is to implement a concept that has been conceived and vetted by others (the founders) – and to do this quickly before financial resources are used up. Because you are often dealing with the same people (professors, assistants, fellow students) you worked with before, but now you are wearing a different hat, conflicts are pre-programmed.

This problem is particularly acute if the founder comes from a social milieu where business thinking is foreign and suspect. Such a person experiences role conflict, which he can survive only at great personal sacrifice. Many people in my social and professional circles have well-thought-out, innovative concepts as well as the intellectual capabilities to implement them, but they sense instinctively – and correctly – that they would suffer personal conflicts which would make the effort too costly.

The Austrian writer Marie von Ebner-Eschenbach (1830-1916), famous for her *Aphorisms*, once wrote, "Our greatest cowardice is that we want to be loved by everyone." While I agree with her observation, her interpretation strikes me as extreme. It is our human nature, not cowardice, that we want to be liked, especially by our friends and acquaintances. One young founder gave me this reason for her failure: "I just couldn't stand being the boss anymore." This is very human – but is it cowardice?

No. Because of this natural inclination we all have, I urge founders *not* to hire friends, acquaintances and fellow students. Or at the very least, founders should anticipate certain sources of conflict and agree on how to handle them.

More than a few friendships have been shattered by such tensions.

To return to our main argument: no one is questioning that business administration is necessary. Business administration offers valuable instruments that have been tested and proven themselves. The issue here is only whether it is the *founder* who should always be burdened with these tasks, or whether a division of labor would be better, given the scope and complexity that modern business administration presents for the non-economist.

The opportunities for a highly developed country like Germany lie in new and forward-looking ideas. Tens of thousands of "Masters of Business Administration" are leaving our institutions of higher education. Where are the "Masters of New Ideas"? We should not discourage the few we have, or the even smaller number brave enough to start a new company, and we should not turn them into business administration dilettantes.

And for all these reasons, we should abandon the primacy of business administration when potential founders come looking for advice.

5.5 Follow the simplest business principles

Experienced practitioners will object that it is very important for founders to be frugal with their resources and not, for example, regard the cash register receipts as surplus and use them rashly for expenditures that are not absolutely necessary. This is certainly an accurate description of the naïveté of many founders. But do you learn thriftiness by acquiring business administration techniques? Frugality is an important virtue. But since when are virtues derived from instruction? Do class materials bring about more virtuous behavior?

Frugality is important, but business administration neither invented it, nor does it induce more frugal behavior. Handling resources wisely and recognizing liquidity problems in a timely fashion are not things that must necessarily be learned through business administration techniques. If these techniques are easy for you, you will find them to be a valuable tool, but you shouldn't hesitate to employ homemade means or outside help as well. This applies, mind you, to the start-up phase of a company, especially when you have a simple but compelling business model.

The slum children in Manila, whose business behavior my colleague Jürgen Zimmer and I observed, could neither read nor write. And certainly not do math. At least that is what their teachers and social workers told us. But when they sold tourists cigarettes and chewing gum from the hawker's trays around their necks, they made correct change to the peso. How were they able to do that? It will forever remain a mystery to their teachers. The American teacher Herndon reported about one pupil who had failed his math class. One evening he ran into him working as a helper at a bowling alley where he was calculating the bowlers' scores with lightning rapidity and total accuracy. Such examples have been described frequently in the literature.

Expertise is not always acquired by established methods. Mathematics is a good example. A preeminent discipline and the cornerstone for all modern science, it allows you to express certain relationships with the utmost precision and clarity. Nonetheless, for most ordinary people the effort required by the mathematical form is greater than the insight gained through this means of expression. While a small segment of our fellow humans finds the mathematical mode of expression simpler and clearer, apparently this is not the case for the majority of us. We understand better when the facts are described to us in words.

The situation is similar for business administration. It is invaluable for complex interrelationships. But what does it do for the ordinary person? The head of the University Clinic in Hannover told the newspaper *Die Zeit*: "As a physician, one can quickly acquire the little bit of business administration that is necessary...." Half of what is taught in business administration relates to things so trivial that one could understand them without it, and the other half is so complex that it doesn't yield any benefit.[41]

Mark Twain, well known for his insight into young people, and also a knowledgeable entrepreneur, addressed this topic over a century ago. He warned founders about getting involved with traditional economists. He had the worst opinion of bankers. "A banker is a person who lends you an umbrella when the sun is shining and wants it back the minute it begins to rain." Such a conventional, play-it-safe mentality is incompatible with new, unconventional ideas.

Anita Roddick, the founder of Body Shop, was of the same opinion. "A bank manager is just about the last person you should ask for advice in business matters because he is only the person who administers the money, a steward if you will. For him it is always a question of percentages, profit and loss; he will never address the *idea*, much less get enthusiastic about it."[42]

Entrepreneurship and business administration do not get along well together. One builds on new ideas and unconventionality, and the other seeks order and may be the enemy of ideas that are out of the mainstream.

5.6 Make room for different ideas

Nothing against business administration. It is necessary. Business administration teaches techniques that are tried and true. But they must be applied in a way that leaves room for new and different concepts. Anyone who comes with committed, precise ideas that are at all different has a hard time resisting conventional business advice. If I had listened to the consultants and bankers, there wouldn't have been any Tea Campaign.

It's as if they want to take an enthusiastic engineer and turn him into a bookkeeper or salesperson. They are not doing him any favors to have him dabbling in a challenging area foreign to his gifts. Accepting the economic calculus is indispensible, but this is not the same as mastering a difficult set of tools designed for another purpose.

If you don't watch out, business administration will triumph over a sound, original concept. But there will be consequences. If I yank the teeth out of a concept, it will be toothless – as in the following story.

5.7 The adventure restaurant

The year is 1986. My colleague Jürgen Zimmer and I have been charged with developing a new kind of school in the Philippines. New, "productive community schools" are supposed to help street kids to earn a living by themselves and to teach them academic subjects more or less as a by-product: learning as a process, not through a predefined curriculum. Jürgen had set up the contacts with the local partners, and I came on as an economist and entrepreneurship expert.

On the Philippine side, the teachers and social workers hired were mostly members of left-leaning organizations. Thus we constantly had to deal with committees, with bureaucrats. Meetings were time-consuming, and ultimately they revolved around a kind of litmus test whether our project followed their political lines.[43]

5.7.1 Entrepreneurship and political dogma

We didn't have the right political "smell." I came to the project essentially to develop practical entrepreneurial ideas with street kids. Jürgen, too, wanted get into the practical work, but any progress was hard-won.

After we managed somehow to pass the political inspections, another hurdle awaited us. The idea that young people could become successful small businesspeople pursuing micro-entrepreneurship was incompatible with local beliefs. The work of Muhammad Yunus or Hernando de Soto was unknown, or rejected as politically suspect, dismissed as "neo-liberal." Yunus demonstrated that women in the villages of Bangladesh, even under the most adverse conditions, could successfully start small businesses using microcredits. For Peru, de Soto described how the greatest impediments to successful economic activity for the poor were bureaucratic barriers and lack of access to the market that shunted them into illegal sectors with no future.

We sensed that the goal was actually not qualifying children for successful economic activity, but rather a certain political consciousness-raising. The message young people kept receiving was something like: "By yourself you don't have a chance. You are a nothing." Naturally this was expressed more politely and with a helpful gesture, but the real point was clear: only with the help of our political organization can you change your life.

At this point it's not important to me whether their political approach was right or wrong . What was important to me was the message to the young people. For me the implicit message that "you are a nothing" is devastating. Our young people were very well qualified to earn their own living without outside help. You could point to a whole list of characteristics in which they were clearly superior to middle-class children of the same age. They had an enormous instinct for good business and spoke bits and pieces of a number of languages – learned, of course, not in school but on the street. To be sure, the street kids weren't able to write correctly, and they didn't have a basic foundation in mathematics, but they had a unique and genuinely admirable life skill: to be able to take care of themselves at a young age, completely on their own.

Even if the political argument were correct, educational measures envisioned for such a population would have to build up young people's self-confidence, would have to recognize existing skills as well as genuine needs, instead of disqualifying from the start the assets these young people already possessed.

5.7.2 Learning outside of the classroom

Another front opened up. We wanted to get started in a practical way and viewed the children's learning processes as connected to, and growing out of, their daily life. The local teachers and social workers, however, wanted the curriculum first and then some practical implementation. It took a while before we recognized that we were threatening their self-image. The pedagogues and social workers were not at all prepared for helping the children learn to earn a better living. It took all of our skill and our professorial status to convince them that learning can take place outside of the classroom and the curriculum.

Turn the children of the poor into businesspeople? In our opinion they already were in business. If we wanted to benefit them, it would be done sooner by sharpening their economic skills, giving them general knowledge and showing them the way out of the informal, often illegal sectors, into regular markets where they could earn more money. Not to establish a charity with donations for the poor, but rather to undertake something that aimed at sustained participation and opportunities in the market.

Finally, we thought, we could start with the practical implementation. Not that we had been particularly impatient – the project extended over several years. The street kids had long been on our side. I had already worked out a first project with them. We wanted to catch the rugged little fish in the filthy oil-laden canals of the city, where they could barely survive, and sell them in aquariums.

I already had gathered experience at Chiang Mai University with this kind of fish, the guppies popular with local tropical fish breeders. They bred well even in small aquariums. The children were also familiar with the fish and were constantly asking when things were going to get started. But nothing was happening with the teachers and social workers. It was no doubt beneath their revolutionary dignity to be involved with small fry.

5.7.3 The idea

Fortunately not all ideas ended like that. One in particular took shape – the adventure restaurant. A group of young people from Mabini Street, a well-known Manila red light district, thought it up. Their basic idea was that the customers came from far and wide and were looking for adventure, so you had to offer them something adventurous. Food, for example. A campfire could be burning in a corner of the restaurant, where you would be able to broil your own steak. Hungry customers could crank their own Italian spaghetti through a noodle machine. In the Filipino part you could catch your own fish and lobsters out of a big basin.

Next to the restaurant, the young people thought, there should be a school for artists, and the restaurant itself should have a stage. Here they could perform acrobatics and theatrical pieces, dance and sing. That was the concept, and not a bad one either. There had never been anything like this before, so this was giving them a real competitive advantage. Moreover, through the young people and their unjaded imagination the restaurant had a good chance of being authentic and lively. And you could also expect a certain sympathy factor that would help the business get publicity and gain customers.

Which entrepreneur should create the restaurant based on this concept? Obviously, the young people themselves. But no, the pedagogues decided that an adult had to put in charge, to guide, to lead and to implement the idea with them.

It wasn't easy to find someone who could – and would – implement someone else's idea, not to mention an idea conceived by street kids. We looked for a long time. Finally we found Imee Castaneda, Dean of the Business Administration Department at Trinity College in Manila – a business management expert; it sounded good.

How do you guide a restaurant to success? You apply what you learned in business administration! OK, you draw up a high marketing budget. What constitutes a restaurant that aims to compete with middle-class restaurants? The answer is obvious: it has to be clean, the help has to be neatly dressed and, of course, the food preparation must look hygienic. So our street kids were put into uniforms similar to what they would wear for confirmation. They were taught to place the fork on the left and the knife to the right. The girls had to make a little curtsy to the guests, and so on, and so forth.

5.7.4 Getting rid of the fanciful ideas

And where was the campfire? Much too dangerous. The artistic performances? Could you do a somersault in your confirmation suit? Any fanciful ideas had been taken away from the children before they were even aware of it. The concept of the adventure restaurant was dead on arrival.

There had to be an intervention. Things couldn't go on like that. Remove Ms. Castaneda? Replace an adult with a teenager? Give the young people's fantasies free rein instead of following proven management formulas? Jürgen and I argued night after night. An intervention by professors who wanted to show the natives how entrepreneurship worked? Once again, two experts from the West who think they really know what it's all about? The end result? No intervention. To echo the words of Karl Valentin, a great German comic actor of yesteryear: we surely would have liked to do it, but we didn't dare to give ourselves permission.

Managed in accordance with business administration principles, was the restaurant a success?

It opened on February 14, 1992. The impression the children made in their confirmation suits was awkward and inauthentic. That they spent their nights sleeping with their parents under a bridge had to be kept secret. The potential advantage of this restaurant as compared with countless other restaurants had been turned into a disadvantage. What could be done? Support and goodwill actions were the watchwords of the day. Media contacts were exploited. Everyone's colleagues, friends and acquaintances were invited to come to the restaurant. The public was informed and also called upon to participate in the "good cause."

The action yielded a lot of public attention for the project – and proved that you can move a dead horse. But only so far. The enormous goodwill that we were able to mobilize helped for a while. Even President Cory Aquino visited the restaurant. But you can't survive on goodwill alone without a convincing concept. Despite the great commitment of all the participants, the restaurant was an economic failure. It suffered an exemplary death: death by conventional economic thinking, with no room for the original imaginations of the Filipino street kids. In 1994 the adventure restaurant was finally laid to rest.

6 Building a business with components

We have argued that the process of developing an entrepreneurial design is similar to composing a piece of music; it is a process in which you continue to hone, polish and refine until everything is in tune and every false note has been eliminated. The image of the composer fits our analogy in yet another way. As we understand the concept of entrepreneurship, we can take advantage of prefabricated components in the same way we put together melodies to create a musical whole. We actually "compose" a company.

6.1 Launching a company – live!

From long years of experience I know that people without a background in business cannot imagine how to put their ideas into practice – that is, how to start a company – without the prior study of business administration. As a result I have given a lot of thought to how one could address this issue convincingly and in a way that leads to direct experience, to dispel the understandable fears that are stirred up again and again by conventional business advice. We've also worked on this problem in our project workshops at the Free University of Berlin.

> Talking about music
> is like dancing about architecture.
>
> STEVE MARTIN
> Actor

Let's imagine a television program: "Launch your own business – Live!" There will be some similarities to the popular German program "*Wetten, dass...*" ["Want to bet..."]. Although we'll have to use our imagination here, our program will be totally realistic, and even more entertaining than Thomas Gottschalk's TV success.

Three would-be business founders will step up to the plate; each one is selected based on the quality of his or her concept.

- Founder A has done the research and determined what goes into making good soap. He has identified sources of supply for ready-made soap (or alternatively, where he can have such soap made). He plans to offer the soap without individual packaging in economical 20-bar boxes.

  Motto: rationality rules.
- Founder B was irritated at how outrageously expensive state-of-the-art variable focus lenses are when purchased from an optician. She had to pay 1198 Euro for hers. After extensive research she finds that she can offer glasses like this for only 169 Euro.

  Motto: make the expensive affordable.
- Founder C has noticed that salt from the Red Sea is beneficial for many types of skin problems, and has identified a number of sources of supply.

  Motto: a healthier life for everyone.

All three candidates have straightforward ideas that are not complex; their sources of supply are on the Internet. They have compared offers by various suppliers and decided on the one that was most advantageous. Our founders have a worked-out concept.

Now it's a matter of implementation. They have to launch their company, set up an office, establish bookkeeping and accounting systems and make arrangements to ship their products. Here we can observe how easy it is to establish a company in today's world.

1. The camera zooms in on our start-up entrepreneurs as they use the Internet to set up a limited liability company as the legal form for their business. For example, the company *Go Ahead* offers this service and will handle all the bureaucratic details for them. (And later, if their concepts prove to be successful and our entrepreneurs need more capital, they can convert this low-cost limited company business form into a more sophisticated legal form.)
2. As the next step our start-up entrepreneurs must set up an office, perhaps using Holger Johnson's *ebuero*. The camera reveals that less than five minutes later a secretary is already answering the telephone in the name of the new company.
3. Our entrepreneurs then call an e-commerce supplier to manage the new company's ordering system.
4. Next, our entrepreneurs contract with an established service provider to handle shipping logistics.

All the basic bureaucratic requirements necessary to launch a business are taken care of in this first phase, which takes only about an hour – during which not a single expensive business consultant, attorney, or finance officer is to be seen.

We now come to customer contact.

The audience is permitted to bet on which of the three ideas has the best prospect of success.

5. The entrepreneurs now set up an order page that they can call up in final form from their e-commerce contractor. Behind this page is the software for a full online shop that is integrated with an accounting system and handles all the administrative work for our entrepreneurs.

And from this moment forward the TV viewers can order the products!

On three status bars, the audience follows the number of orders received. Whoever gets the most orders wins.

This could be the start of a mass movement: entrepreneurship for everyone! Not only can the founders of these businesses become successful entrepreneurs right out of the gate, but the audience also learns how they themselves could launch a business. It's like watching an instructional film, but much more exciting. The economic incentive is enormous. With this initial start-up, even if it only appeals to a few hundred buyers, the company is already worth something; an enterprise value has been created.

Entrepreneurship as a new popular sport?!

6.2 Working with components

The composer did not learn to play every instrument, just as today the captain of a ship is not a machinist, software specialist and navigation expert all rolled into one. What is critical is a general mastery of the tools in order to be able to assemble them in new combinations and to be able to adjust and coordinate the individual instruments, rather than a total mastery of each individual instrument. We can imagine the entrepreneur as a composer who envisions a goal and who understands how to use his instruments. Until now we have rarely encountered "composers" like this as founders. However, this is the simplest way to launch a start-up – with professional components from the very beginning.

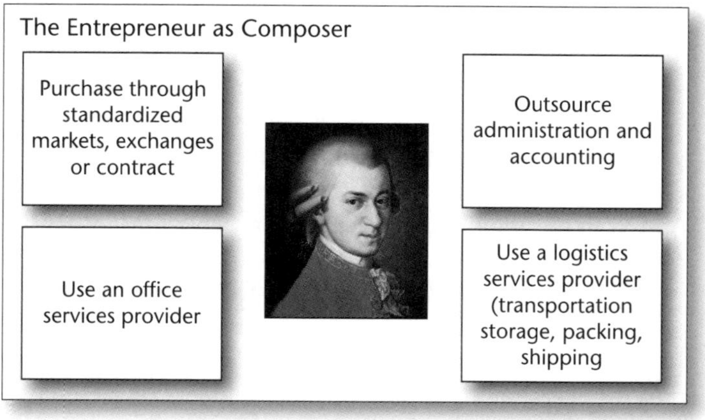

I've chosen the figure of the composer because successful entrepreneurs often don't invent anything new, but rather take things that already exist and recombine them in a different way, that is, they assemble existing components to create something new.

The founders of Skype demonstrated this in the hi-tech sector. Skype uses a standard technology that has been known for years, thereby competing with the big telecommunications companies, but at prices far below theirs. [44] The company's key innovation lay not in developing its own product, but rather in the user-friendly development and improvement of interfaces. Measured against the standards of new technological developments, this is a relatively meager achievement – but with a prodigious economic result.[45] Skype is an example of how the results of a creative concept start-up can shatter all previous conceptions of value creation. This dramatic example clearly demonstrates the potential impact of creative concept start-ups.

6.2.1 Start-ups with wings

Sometimes it's necessary to make a radical break with familiar ideas. The dream of flying is probably as old as mankind itself. Until about 1890 all attempts to fly were based on observing birds in flight and devising constructions that imitated the flight of birds, that is, apparatuses with movable wings. All struggled with the problem of making those wings strong enough to compensate for the weight of humans.

The breakthrough for flying came about very differently, with *fixed* wings. It was fixed wing construction that succeeded in working with either *pull* (propellers) or later with *push* (jet engines).

Let's draw an analogy. The prevailing notion is that a company is a tangible entity made up of buildings, staff, and workplaces. It makes products or provides services. This requires organization and management.

For the moment let's erase the notion of "company" from our brains. We can now approach the subject of "founding" a business very differently. The question we must ask ourselves is: What *new entity* can I create out of the many components that already exist? Whether this new business will require premises, whether it will need a staff, and what resources will be necessary – all these questions remain open at first. The crucial work is taking place in your head. What is critical is discovering new combinations and more efficient processes – in any possible mix you can imagine – using the building blocks that are available to you, a kit that's growing by the day in terms of the number and variety of its components.

Economists may prefer to explain this paradigm change through the theory of transaction costs. In the past, in light of the high transaction costs it made sense to keep most activities within the company. These days, however, because of increasing specialization and the low cost of communications, you can take advantage of pre-existing components outside the company.

The "company" that is the theme of this book consists of the intellectual agility required to fit external components into a concept. What remains as the management task is coordinating these components and harmonizing them with one another.

This is possible under the technological and organizational conditions that are evolving today, and thinking in terms of a *virtual* company will become something we'll take completely for granted.

The old question was, "What do I need to establish my company and organize it successfully?" The new question is, "What new thing can I compose out of modules that already exist?"

6.2.2 An Example

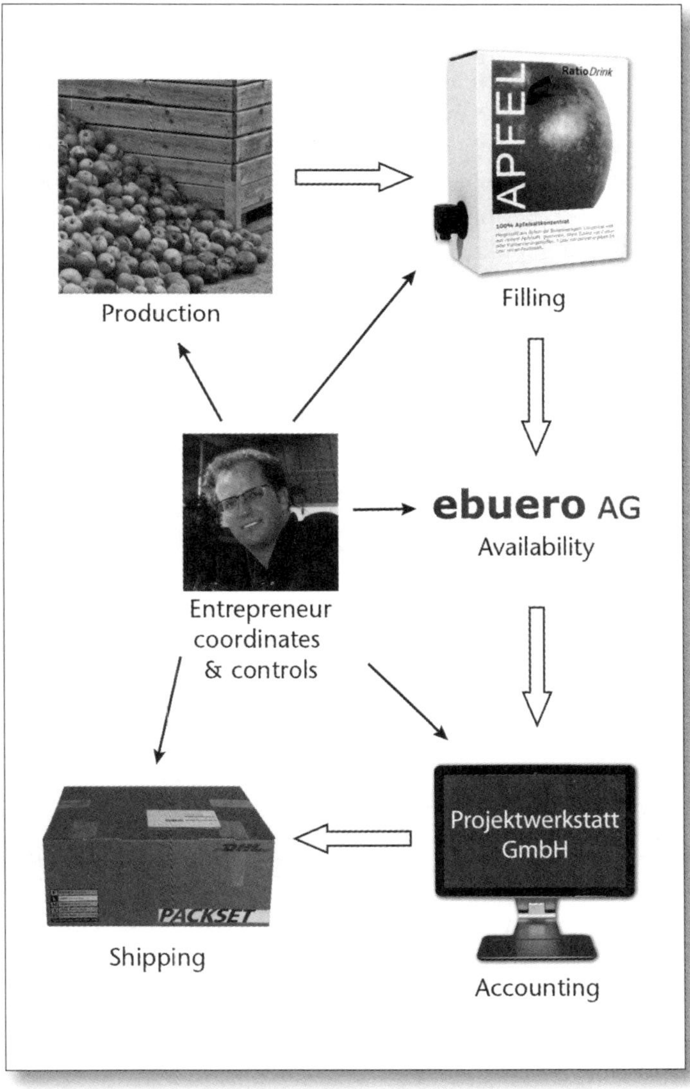

A start-up created out of components: let's use *RatioDrink AG* as an example.

The diagram illustrates the components of a company modeled on the already-mentioned *RatioDrink*. Moving clockwise from the upper left, the apple juice concentrate is purchased from the producers and put into 3-liter bag-in-box containers at a filling plant. *ebuero* takes the orders, and all bookkeeping tasks are handled by *Projektwerkstatt*. Shipping is also outsourced.

All the components mentioned here are offered by professional operations or by professional service providers.

In a model like this the founders' job involves: (1) conceiving a concept that can be put together from components; (2) finding partners who offer these components at a professional level; (3) coordinating and controlling the interplay of these components.

You can see immediately what tremendous advantages the component model offers:

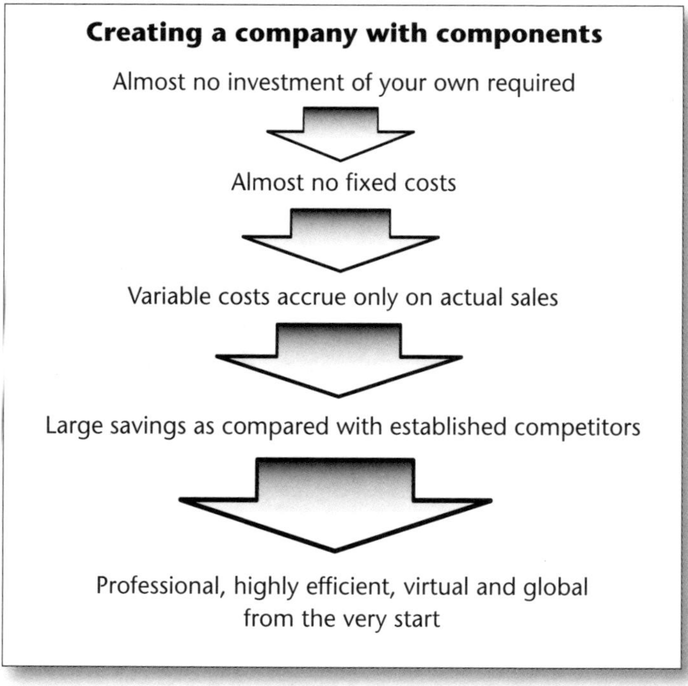

Instead of making you into an overworked small business owner, this model transforms you into a *powerful entrepreneur*. Almost no investment is necessary. Your operation functions at a highly professional level from the very beginning. As a rule, variable costs arise only if actual orders are received. You don't have a large administrative apparatus that you must set up and finance. Instead, you are professional and highly efficient from the start because your components are provided by experienced partners who themselves have already achieved economies of scale. Compare for yourself the contrast between this and starting a company in the conventional manner with respect to the financial expenses, risks and workload for the founders.[46]

Professional support for founders is an absolute necessity. Studies of successful start-ups highlight repeatedly how important is the division of roles among the lead entrepreneur and the professional management team. The founder as lead entrepreneur must be able to concentrate fully on the concept and its further development, while the management must handle the day-to-day business operations.

If a founder cannot establish this type of professional support, his start-up concept is, in my opinion, not workable. This does not necessarily mean that you need large amounts of capital for start-ups. "Workable" means that the concept is distinguished by clearly identifiable market advantages that will permit the business to attract customers and generate the revenue it needs to pay for professional staff. Anyone who believes that he cannot afford professionals should give it a try with "unprofessionals!"

If you are now in the mood to jump up and get started, armed with your laptop: go for it! You are not reading a novel, an economic fiction; you are firmly based in reality, with both feet on the ground.

6.2.3 The company as an idea construct

What all this amounts to is a permanent break with tradition, a change in the way businesses are viewed. Up to now attention has been focused almost exclusively on resources. How much capital did the company have at its disposal? What manufacturing facilities, what machinery did it have? The term *human capital* reveals the extent to which capital has been the starting point for any analysis. Even people were regarded as a form of capital, as a resource. Human capital, so to speak, was merely a dimension of the capital required to operate a business.

This is the *resource-based view of the firm.*

But the balance has shifted. These days you can launch a business without the traditional resources. Now, increasingly, the sum total of the ideas and their realization is what matters. Today we can regard companies as idea constructs.

Which of the ideas flowing into its products make up the strength of a company? How much public esteem does the company enjoy? With what attitudes or by what actions has the company been able to garner goodwill for itself? How did it succeed in winning the hearts and minds of its employees (instead of sending them to motivation workshops)? What concepts will determine the company's future competitiveness? What will make it difficult for imitators to become a danger to the company?

In the past, the size of the company as expressed in its economies of scale was a decisive advantage. Today,even large companies can get into trouble overnight because they relied too heavily on their resources, their superior capitalization and their market position.

"At the beginning of every big company was a small idea," notes Peter Drucker. Does this mean that at the end, after the company has grown large, there will be big ideas? Or do large organizations, with big bureaucracies, tend to suppress new ideas? Could it be that large size and originality are not compatible? Are large organizations more inhospitable to employees' unconventional, offbeat and unorthodox ideas than small, young organizations would be? Could it be that the call for *corporate entrepreneurship*, that is, the solicitation of more entrepreneurial initiatives within a company, is itself a sign of a company's creeping bureaucratization that follows increasing company size?

This doesn't mean that resources are unimportant, but that they are becoming less significant. An approach that emphasizes only resources is increasingly missing real possibilities. What we need in addition to resources is an *idea-based view of the firm.*

6.3 Eliminating growth crises

Our component model has yet another significant advantage.

It is well known that young firms pass through several stages in which the company is often plunged into crises.[47] Each growth stage creates its own crisis, in which management must react quickly to a newly emerging business situation, and the reaction to each looming crisis lays the foundation for the next crisis. If the right reaction does not occur, the company will be threatened with ruin.

A study covering the years 1983 through 2002 concluded that the insolvency rate for start-ups is particularly high during the first six years. In fact, only about 50 percent survive until year six. As the reasons for this the authors cite limited company size and lack of experience.[48] Market newcomers tend to start with companies that are too small (*liability of smallness*).[49]

In the light of these facts, we can see how establishing a new business using components reduces the start-up risks. When we make use of components, we avail ourselves of established, experienced entities that operate on a large, efficient scale.

In the initial phase management issues are not yet a problem. The founders more or less keep to themselves. Communications are informal, adequate and uncomplicated. The style is collegial. The founders and the staff, which is still small, are highly motivated and perform their duties willingly and generously. At this early stage customer contact likewise remains direct and unproblematic.[50]

If growth continues, new staff will be hired, and the old informal working style will become problematic. Moreover, the new staff members will be less enthusiastic. The company requires stricter management. Without it, a "pioneer crisis" threatens. The founders, frustrated by the new management demands, look back on the "good old days" with nostalgia. They cling to the informal style of the start-up phase, which now produces strife among the founders. It becomes necessary to transition to a professional management team organized along functional lines.[51]

With further growth, the next crisis emerges. Operations become more centralized, and top management is divorced from day-to-day operations. Organizational units and managers are frustrated and demand a greater voice. The "autonomy crisis" has arrived. The response is decentralization, in which the lower levels are given more authority. Continued growth brings on the next challenge: top management fears losing control, subsystems become independent, and centrifugal forces are released. A "control crisis" threatens.

In this phase of a company's growth it becomes necessary to establish control mechanisms; horizontal project groups are formed and more complex forms of organization established. The result is more red tape. Jurisdictional disputes arise more frequently and administrative work grows disproportionately. The "bureaucracy crisis" is at the door.[52]

According to Schreyögg, companies fail mostly as a result of management errors. Founders systematically underestimate management problems. This assessment is supported by the fact that re-starts are more successful than first-starts. From these typical growth crises, Schreyögg concludes that professionalization of management is crucial.

For start-up entrepreneurs these empirical observations are highly valuable, *but only if they establish a company in the conventional manner*.

But what if they launch a business using components? With components, they are buying professionalism from the very start. From day one they work on an efficient operational scale and with a higher degree of professionalism. The crises mentioned above won't even come up. There is simply no basis for them. And this significantly increases a new venture's likelihood of survival.

This method provides yet another crucial advantage for the founders: now they can concentrate on the entrepreneurial design and develop it further, instead of exhausting themselves with the day-to-day administrative tasks. Professionally delivered components make up for the inexperience typical of many founders. Business consulting entities could take on a new and valuable role – identifying experienced, professional companies suitable to be used as components.

An examination of the typical growth crises also shows that there is a clear advantage to putting a simple entrepreneurial design into effect, because most of the crisis manifestations are the result of increasing complexity.

Get big, but remain small

The principle is "Get big, but remain small." This is the advantage of making use of large, efficient units without having to establish and operate them yourself. Your company grows, but the core activity that you control remains small, and thus coherent and manageable.

6.4 Making use of "embedded knowledge"

We have already seen that the majority view considers the founding idea not a significant factor for the success of a newly founded business. "In entrepreneurship, ideas are really a dime a dozen."[53] Venture capitalists play the same tune when they choose a first-class team with a second-class idea over a first class idea with a second-class team.

What's correct about this perspective is that you don't need an idea on the magnitude of Bill Gates's plan for Microsoft in order to be able to start a successful new venture. But to draw the opposite conclusion, that a constitutive idea has only minor importance in the launch of a business, ignores the potential of creative concept start-ups. Is the idea really of secondary importance?

> [It is important] to have a great idea and to pursue it with a passion. You can be successful even if the most promising doctoral students, the most famous universities and companies do not believe in your project in their wildest dreams.
>
> STEVE WOZNIAK,
> Apple co-founder

Let's look at the topic of "implementation" a little more closely and from a different perspective than before.

Imagine the following scenario: you're a businessman and you have the idea of buying low-priced goods in Madeira and selling them at high prices in your domestic market. That's the founding idea. What's critical for the idea to be a success? The answer seems clear: the implementation.

You need a ship. You must know how to sail, and sail well. The ship must have been built with care. You know the requirements for your crew and you recruit your personnel carefully. You have the knowledge and experience required to lead a crew, even under difficult conditions. You've familiarized yourself with the route and its many hazards and hardships. You've purchased supplies and are guiding your ship along the routeresponsibly and with expertise. A multiplicity of considerations and judgments are necessary, and whether you'll ultimately reach your goal depends on you, your crew, your ship, your collective expertise, weighing all the foreseeable risks and perhaps a little bit of luck.

Obviously, in this example the idea pales in comparison with the difficulties inherent in its implementation. Isn't this clear proof that it all comes down to the implementation? And don't these considerations sound as if they could easily be applied to the position of a business that has to steer through difficult situations in the market and competition, where leadership, products and staff are crucial, and where the prudence with which this organization must confront setbacks and unanticipated situations is needed on a daily basis? The analogy seems so obvious. But is it really? Does a modern businessman wanting to buy goods from far-away Madeira still have to go about getting ship, crew and handling all the details a project like this entails for himself?

Of course not. Our scenario is not from our own times, but from a bygone era. Today an entrepreneur is no longer obliged to concern himself with all these details. A modern businessman works with service packages that are standardized and include many types of expertise that in the past he himself would have to have mastered and put into practice. But today he is free to ignore many of the aspects traditionally involved in implementation.

The fact that we can assemble components to start a business changes the problem of implementation radically – both quantitatively and qualitatively. Implementation can be delegated to professionals through the choice of components. Implementation is now reduced to combining components.

We can call this "embedded knowledge," that is, the knowledge we have at our disposal when we make use of such components. When we use a clock to tell the time, we are relying on the function of a complicated mechanism as it has developed over centuries at the hands of highly skilled craftsmen. One may regret that we no longer have the knowledge of all the details, as perhaps a collector of old watches does, but we are much more efficient when we make use of this embedded knowledge without having learned all its details for ourselves.

The first step is to have an idea and to work on it until a compelling concept emerges. The second step is to find pre-existing professional components with which you can bring the idea to life in all its artistic details.

Concept plus components

A carefully thought-out concept plus professional components – that is the magic formula with which we can challenge the major players of the economic world.

7 Playing in the Big Boys' League

7.1 Can You Imagine Building an Industrial Facility?

I'm sitting in a plane headed for Asia. My seatmate, as it turns out in conversation, works in industry, at the large German conglomerate ThyssenKrupp. His assignment is to coordinate the construction of a cement factory in Saraburi, north of Bangkok. I listen to him attentively, but naturally my thoughts are full of launching businesses using components. I take a deep breath and ask, "This might sound totally absurd to you, but can I tell you how I, as a layman, would build a cement factory?" He says nothing, so I continue: "I'd look for an engineering firm that has the know-how and experience building cement factories. And then I would ask them to buy all the parts you need for a cement factory, that is, the machinery, conveyor belts and everything else you'd need, wherever these things can be bought on the best terms. The engineering firm would have to put the parts together or coordinate the construction. What do you think of that? But please – since I know nothing about cement except that I've seen bags of it, be very candid. What do you think of the idea?" My seatmate responded very calmly, "In principle we don't do it any differently than what you've described. We get an engineering firm, we already have the one we're going to work with, and then, generally speaking, we get everything we need from all over the world. Naturally, the parts we can make ourselves, we get in-house." "Please," I say, "another silly question. Won't the whole thing be less expensive if *I* build it than if a big company does?" "Of course you're cheaper," he says. "You're not saddled with the whole apparatus we're forced to finance. The Chinese we built a cement factory for are now doing it this way too. Now they're our competition in Dubai." "Listen," I say somewhat concerned, "what does this mean for ThyssenKrupp?" There's a short pause, then he says, "I'll be retiring in a year and a half."

7.2 Buying a Service Package

If even you can build an industrial facility, then you can do a lot of other things, too. We don't have to start off with a cement factory.

These days many things come bundled in a service package that can be purchased ready-to-go. For example, a single telephone call to the shipping offices of *Deutsches Seekontor* was enough to get tea from Calcutta to Berlin. I merely had to give them the Calcutta address where the tea was stored and a delivery address in Germany. Hapag-Lloyd or some other shipping company would provide the expertise and take on all the other responsibilities – the quality of the ship and container, training and duties of the captain, choice of international sea route, details of warehousing, loading the ship in Calcutta and processing in Hamburg, including the customs paperwork. This system turns you into an "importer," and now you can devote yourself to the *why* and *how* of selling your tea.

In the old days, if a merchant wanted to purchase Egyptian cotton, he had to have the quality checked on site in Cairo. Then he had to arrange payment, shipping, export, import into his own country and paying the customs duties, just to mention a few of the most important steps. A lot could go wrong in the process. You had to find trustworthy business partners, but even then the risks remained high and difficult to predict. Getting launched as a newcomer was extremely difficult, if not impossible. The business not only required lots of money and experience, but it took years, if not generations, for it to grow to a size that permitted it to operate successfully in the international sphere.

Today you can buy a cotton contract on the New York Mercantile Exchange. The quality level is precisely defined; you can rely on compliance with basic terms like quantity, quality, agreed-upon price and the subsequent settlement of the transaction. Payment transactions are likewise standardized and reliable. What was previously a bold and expensive undertaking is now very manageable and can be set up with only a few telephone calls. What you previously had to do for yourself, at great risk, you can now delegate. You can outsource these tasks and transact business with much lower inherent risk.

This is the critical difference from the world of yesterday. In a modern economic system you can think and act in ready-to-go components, while in the past it was necessary to master a multiplicity of complex processes and risks. But this isn't all; the system also gives you access to a playing field where the big boys don't operate any differently than you do.

7.3 Compose Your Company

Let's start with a small, manageable example.

Rafael Kugel explains:

Scientists at the University of Essen discovered that the process of removing the rapeseed's bitter hull made it possible to extract pleasant-tasting oil. The valuable properties of rapeseed oil, now more commonly known as canola oil, have long been known, and the German Society for Nutrition (Deutsche Gesellschaft für Ernährung) expressly recommends its consumption because of its nutritional benefits: it contains 60% monounsaturated fatty acids and high levels of vitamin E, as well as polyunsaturated omega-3 and omega-6 fatty acids. After the discovery of how to make the oil palatable, I thought it would be possible to help canola oil achieve a new economic life. If you packaged this oil in large containers and marketed it directly to the consumer, instead of selling it over the counter in small containers at high prices, wouldn't that convince consumers to buy their canola oil by mail order from me? The Tea Campaign model transferred to canola oil?

My calculations showed that I could offer high-quality organic cold-pressed oil at almost half the customary price. I would have to create a webpage of my own, but I didn't want to have to deal with the daily administration of my little business. Internet orders are directed to and processed by the Projektwerkstatt company's ordering system. Filling the canola oil into 3-liter bag-in-box containers is handled by a professional packager in Hamburg, one who also prepares the orders for shipping and delivers them to the post office parcel service. This type of specialized division of labor has decisive advantages. Although at present my company still does a relatively small volume of business, I am working with the technology and thus the efficiency of the "big boys." This means that without a major investment of my own I can play in the big leagues with established companies – efficiently, professionally, and at a cost far lower than if I took over all these tasks myself. Costs are incurred only if there are orders to be processed. Thus my risk of failing due to high fixed costs in conjunction with too few orders is very small. But above all, my mind is free for true executive functions, such as ongoing monitoring of outsourced activities, fine-tuning my concept, or contacts with the media.

Established in August 2005, my business reached the break-even point after only three weeks because of its low fixed costs. Most startup consultants had predicted that my workday would be up to 14 hours long, but the reality is quite different. Routine activities require no more than half an hour a day. This means there's time left for other important things: my thoughts are already focused on founding that next company.

By the way, I was a failure in the business plan competition – they said my financing plan wasn't realistic.

What are you waiting for? Start to compose your own company.

Can you delegate, compose and outsource everything that was once thought of as implementation differently now? Indeed you can.

The following tiny company established by our serial entrepreneur, Holger Johnson, is the absolute microform of a company that works with components. Once the components have been set up, it functions virtually by itself.

What was the idea for this tiny company? To provide telephone systems with the music that callers listen to while waiting on hold – and to relieve the operators of these telephone systems of the burden of dealing with GEMA, the German performance rights and royalty-collecting organization similar to ASCAP (*American Society of Composers, Authors and Publishers*) in the US. Holger had a CD with appropriate music burned and set up an online shop. Shipping logistics are handled by a service provider. How do the customers find the website? The answer is simple – through search engines. It seems that music for callers on hold is a typical product people look for on the Internet.

What remains is the coordination between the individual service packages, which is handled professionally. Once coordination has been set up and routinized, the job of the entrepreneur is limited to quality control of the individual service packages agreed upon. Thus he gains time to concentrate on his real tasks, *i.e.*, observing the market, reacting to market changes and focusing his attention on wider horizons instead on the day-to-day business.

> We live in a time of perfect means.
>
> ALBERT EINSTEIN

There are components for almost everything, even of very high quality. First, there are professional markets where, until now, the major players have done their purchasing. There are exchanges or auctions with standardized products and standardized levels of quality. But there are also informal structures like Internet platforms that make it possible to gain access to producers, even if they are apparently producing at the other side of the earth. Above all, there are professional service providers who save us the packing and shipping. Not to mention virtually free channels of communication by e-mail, telephone or videoconferencing, which radically improve making contact while minimizing its costs. Basically, we have an enormous toolbox at our disposal, plus an almost limitless number of building blocks, from which we can create an infinite number of new combinations. Just as in the last century Stanislaw Lem composed science fiction novels out of hi-tech elements, today we can write *economic fiction* in which people synthesize their own visions out of an existing tool kit and its components.

> Things fall into composition.
>
> Attributed to the novelist HENRY JAMES (1843-1916)

Production isn't the problem. There's an excess of production capacity. Almost every producer is overjoyed to receive an order. Even brand name manufacturers, if they operate the production themselves, are happy when they can work at full capacity, and are willing to produce items for you, even if you are selling virtually the same product but under your own brand name.

Operating their facility at full capacity is more important to them than competition with some "no-name," which is, of course, what you are. At least at the beginning. Later, when you are conspicuously successful and achieve a market share worthy of note, this may change. But by then you will be large enough and will have long since researched alternatives.

7.4 An Example: Making Toothbrushes Cheaper

Not far from Bonn is a factory that makes most of the toothbrushes sold in Germany. A number of well-known brands have their toothbrushes made for them there. You, too, can have your toothbrushes manufactured there and sell them under your own name or under some other fancy name. Get together with your friends and acquaintances and start a Toothbrush Campaign. You know that toothbrushes should not be used too long; otherwise they will damage your teeth, no matter how expensive or scientific their design. You yourself need at least ten toothbrushes a year. So your own circle of friends and acquaintances is sufficient for a small campaign. Why should your friends buy their toothbrushes from you?

You can already figure it out. Not because you're attractive and likeable and can talk your friends into buying them from you, but because naturally your toothbrushes are much cheaper than the toothbrushes they're buying for themselves, even at the discount store. Materials and production cost almost nothing. Toothbrushes become expensive because of the advertising to develop the brand and sales.

How should you sell your toothbrushes? Set up an online shop so that the acquaintances of your acquaintances can buy a year's supply, or else you can distribute the toothbrushes in person when you go for a visit. Don't be afraid that your friends will laugh at you. They'll only do that at the beginning before they understand the concept. After that, they'll either be green with envy or they'll immediately start looking for a product to use for a little campaign of their own. If you brush your teeth with an electric toothbrush – and we hope you do – the enterprise will pay off that much faster. You've certainly already been irritated at how expensive those little brushes for the top of the handpiece are. Ideally you should sell the motor right along with it. It should be rugged and have a long service life, and the device should be designed with sensor technology that adjusts the pressure on the teeth, which is usually too strong. In this way you'll have eliminated the problem created by brand name electric toothbrush manufacturers, which is that a different toothbrush head must be purchased for every brand of electric toothbrush.

Now you start to think of a brand name. Take "Green" for example. Yes, "Green." You can't call your electric toothbrush "Braun [Brown]" (Braun is the name of a famous German company with a reputation for high-quality products). But "Green," maybe you could. To be safe, look for someone whose name is "Green" and name your company after him. (Keep looking under "Green" in the telephone book until you find someone who is willing to go along with this experiment.) If when you try to register the name, they tell you that the name "Green" isn't allowed, bring a legal action. If the brand "Brown" is allowed, "Green" has to be permitted too. What I'm really trying to say here is that you should choose a memorable name that is as simple as possible and not let yourself be dissuaded too quickly by statements like "That won't work" or "There's one like that already."

The Tea Campaign never had any difficulty buying good quality tea, not even when the tea merchants tried to use their market power against us and attempted to influence tea producers to stop selling to us.

These days production is no longer the problem. So what *is* the problem? Packaging and shipping? This is handled by professional packagers and shippers. The *Projektwerkstatt* offers this service – we already ship more than 100,000 parcels each year. We have the entire infrastructure. Your few dozen or several hundred packages won't make any difference. As far as the costs are concerned, you'll be getting involved with an enterprise that's already operating with extreme efficiency. Even the postage will be cheaper for you. While you'll quickly shell out six Euros for a single package mailed parcel post at the post office, the same package will cost only half as much with us – and you'll save yourself the trip to the post office and the time waiting in line. Obviously the cost of packaging material is also lower because we buy in quantity. It's a real win-win situation. You'll save a lot of money, and we'll utilize our existing capacity more efficiently, and later, when you're sending a thousand packages, our costs will be even lower because now we'll have larger volume and better purchase discounts because of you. But check around to see whether you can find another service provider who might be even cheaper than we are, or who is in a better position to meet your specific needs.

What's left is operating and administering the online shop. Here the solution is even simpler. Set up your own online shop by using software that releases you from all the administrative duties. At the end of the month you'll get a report on how much you've sold and earned. If you're curious and want to check on your business every night, you can call up the latest data yourself any time you want to. Nowadays, you will find professional service providers who offer this service.

What are you waiting for?[54]

7.5 Short of Capital?

Instead of working on their concept idea and fine-tuning it, many founders still think that market success will come through large production volume. This belief is widespread, whether it's because you've heard that the big boys swallow the small fry, or because as an economist you are familiar with economies of scale (*i.e.,* in order to produce cheaply you have to produce in large quantity and that this is the way to beat out the competition in the marketplace). The standard argument made by tinkerers and would-be start-up entrepreneurs is, "If they made my product by the millions, it would be low-cost and competitive in the market." What follows this statement is almost automatic: "What I need is an investor who gives me the millions I need to do this." I, too, often get such requests. My answer is blunt: "I wouldn't give you the capital – even if I had it." Today size alone is not enough, and apparently I'm not the only one who says this. Most other rationally thinking people do, too. You could just as well expect an investor to go to the casino, put two million on Red 17 and hope the roulette will stop at 17 in the next round.

I bring this up only because it helps us better understand the phrase (or perhaps we should say "myth") of the "lack of capital for start-up entrepreneurs."

Now before you throw this book down in disgust, I'll grant you that there are exceptions. When research and development in the hi-tech area is necessary, you will need large amounts of capital. The same holds true in pharmaceutical research. An enormous amount of capital is required from the first research findings through clinical trials to the sale of a drug.

But even today start-ups in these segments represent only a small fraction of the new businesses actually established. This share would be even smaller if we included the many potential start-ups that are obstructed or inhibited these days through misconceptions.

Is there enough capital available for start-up entrepreneurs? These days there is a goodly number of institutions that provide venture capital. Banks have set up departments specializing in this. In my own circles I am not aware of a single case in which a start-up was not undertaken for lack of financial resources. In fact, the opposite is the case. Investors, like venture capital firms or business angels, are actively pursuing promising concepts.

Take a look at the Deutsche Gründer- und Unternehmertage (German Founders' Fair) in Berlin or similar events in other parts of Germany. You'll find an almost inconceivable array of offerings, but scarcely any start-up entrepreneurs. And even fewer good start-up concepts. The situation may have been different a few years ago, but today capital is no longer the bottleneck.[55]

The fact that many start-ups fail due to liquidity problems should not mislead us to draw the wrong conclusion. Cash-flow problems are the final act in a failed start-up, but not necessarily the cause of the failure. When a patient dies, the heart finally stops, but it would be wrong to conclude from this that he must have died from heart failure.

In an information society capital is found in people's brains, and only secondarily in the bank. During the industrial age ideas derived their power from the capital that stood behind them. The pioneer Friedrich Harkort's idea to cover Germany with a network of railroads was a profitable idea in keeping with Germany's economic and logistical situation. Its successful implementation depended on the (enormous) capital resources required. The contemporary counter-example is Skype. Linking up the entire world by Internet telephone required astoundingly little capital.

Today ideas reach their fruition through the efforts of our brains, not through capital. Not because we implement them in the language and techniques of business administration (the way business plans do), but because the ideas are well-conceived, improved, reworked, and maybe even scrapped and replaced with better ideas. Today the laurels are awarded for mental effort, for the ability to think and act unconventionally, for new perspectives and new combinations. And sometimes for the ability to think like an outsider, to be regarded as crazy – and the capacity for enduring this.

Of course, the dinosaurs also win from time to time. Mass has weight, and weight also counts. Some dinosaurs are adaptable and can reinvent themselves. After all, the mass that has accrued also includes the money to buy good brains through high salaries. Is it possible to make them our own? One side says the "war for talent" can be won with money. But according to the other side, new professional standards are developing, standards involving lifestyle and self-realization, criteria that are not always compatible with large organizations. My own observation at the university is that these days students feel much less attracted to the big names in industry than they were in the past.[56]

7.6 Personality, not Anonymity

There are many people who perceive the market and competition as faceless, as a game to be played by the big and the powerful, where brutality prevails and capital and power interests dominate all other values. It's just not their "world." Their aversion is expressed in their lack of interest and scant inclination to involve themselves in the realm of business.

But are these conceptions still correct?

Today size is no longer the be-all and end-all. Flexibility decreases as organizations grow, while bureaucracy increases, and with it the type of manager who would rather let people go than conceptualize something innovative, the type of manager who plays politics without any entrepreneurial vision, who keeps whole divisions applying for government subsidies but fails to recognize fundamental market shifts or notices them only as the crash begins. Not even business school professors believe in the gospel of size any longer. The advantages of large series are not endlessly expandable. On the contrary, size means more complexity, which often results in costs in excess of what higher sales can bring in. Only the managers at conglomerates maintain their steadfast belief in size. Actually, the number of small firms is growing all over the world, and they are also responsible for creating more jobs. In Germany, the number of jobs at big companies has been *declining* continuously since the beginning of the 1980s.

Anyone not convinced by these arguments should read Martin Suter's book *Business Class.*[57] Where departments intrigue against one another, where a manager's chief preoccupation is with solidifying his own position, one has to ask oneself: how are these dinosaurs going to survive in an environment focused increasingly on competition and performance? Skype's two founders taught the telecom giants fear. We have known for some time that innovation and trail-blazing ideas do not commonly originate in large organizations.

And must companies always be impersonal and "unfathomable?" There are other models. A company can also have a face. It can have individuality and reveal the founder's personality and his convictions. The market and competition need not be brutal and faceless. The market can also be a contest of ideas. Today, when founders and small companies enjoy virtually the same access to information and know-how as the major players do, as capital and intrigue are losing their significance in the knowledge society, the rules for success are being re-written.

Gottlieb Duttweiler, founder of the Swiss company Migros, was the first to recognize the signs of a new era. He did battle for good products and low prices with the entire retail industry in his country. He refused to reduce product quality in order to offer his goods at bargain prices. He wanted to keep quality high, but save on transport and packaging in order to eliminate unnecessary expense. His customers understood that. When in January 1926 a phalanx of retailers fought back and undercut his prices in a major dumping campaign, the Zurich housewives saw through the maneuver. Even though they had to wait for Duttweiler's trucks in the icy January weather when they could have made their purchases at lower prices in the warm shops of his competitors, they remained loyal to Duttweiler. If they hadn't, Migros would have disappeared permanently from the scene that first year and Duttweiler would have gone down in the annals of the retail trade as a failure. Without the person of Duttweiler, the success of Migros cannot be explained.

In art it's obvious that the work also reveals the artist, his way of seeing things, her individuality. Success isn't a result of uncritical, abject accommodation to the market and popular taste, but rather of new and different ways of seeing things through the originality of the artist. Can this be transferred to companies?

In the Tea Campaign the customer was not king; instead, the focus was on rationality. If we had accommodated ourselves to the desires of the customer, today we would have a wide assortment of many kinds of tea in small packages, and accordingly the costs and prices would be just as high as those in the conventional tea business.

Perhaps this makes it understandable why even concepts as simple as the one devised by the Migros founder, the Ikea idea and even the Tea Campaign were destined to be such resounding successes. "In the kingdom of the blind, the one-eyed man is king," goes the saying. Where the world of the market is dominated by an obsession with sheer profit maximization, even tiny ideas have great possibilities. From the world of art we know that being business-minded by itself does not necessarily lead to success. Could it be that this also applies to economic life?

7.7 So, now do you want a little company of your own?

"Small is beautiful" – that may be true, you concede. Maybe you are more flexible than the big boys and you're not saddled with a huge administrative apparatus. But doesn't a small company have definite economic handicaps? Small batches, high unit costs, no money for research and development or for marketing?

Marketing and infrastructure have changed in a way that has made the traditional perceptions of large and small obsolete. This is because of the openness and transparency of the modern markets, as well as the new professionalism and process reliability.

Thus, and this is the decisive factor, founders have access to the same market and on practically the same terms as the big companies.

Playing with the big boys

Availability of new infrastructure

Highly developed division of labor

Standardized markets, exchanges and product quality

Availability of professional service providers

Our schools seldom discuss the workings of the commodity exchanges, if they're not even dismissed outright as instruments of speculation. An example of this is the documentary film "September Wheat" [*Septemberweizen*] (1980) by German director Peter Krieg, which is still shown in German schools today. The film singles out from the broad spectrum of business the most speculative area by far, the September deadline for wheat futures trading. Using this extreme example, it suggests that modern exchanges are merely the playthings of speculators, but it fails to recognize the inherent opportunities that arise from the modern trading systems.

So would you like to have a little company of your own?

Buy yourself a heating oil contract at ICE Futures Europe in London. The oil will meet the exact specifications of the DIN standard for German heating oil. A contract means 100 tons of heating oil, that is, 110,000 liters. The broker requires a financial margin of 5% of the amount traded plus a commission of about 1%. Now, for all practical purposes you are trading at approximately the same conditions as Exxon or Shell. Tell your friends and acquaintances that, effective immediately, they can buy their heating oil from you at a pre-set price that will be significantly cheaper than that charged by their heating oil company. At the same time you have to contract with a tanker trucking company to pick up the heating oil at the port of delivery, usually Rotterdam, and then immediately fill the oil tanks of your friends and acquaintances.

The calculation is simple and you'll know it before launching your little campaign. It will be the cost of the oil contract, the broker's commission, cost of shipping, about a dozen phone calls, and a file folder. At first, 110,000 liters may seem like a lot, but in actuality it isn't. The oil tank for a single family home holds 3,000 liters, and often more. Tanks for apartment buildings have a capacity of 30,000 to 50,000 liters, so that just a few agreements with your friends will be enough. (You'll have to make sure that your friends make a binding commitment to actually take the oil, or else you'll need to have a back-up list of prospects.) The first time you'll be totally stressed and you might not sleep well at night. The second time, when you are familiar with the broker's and shipper's rules and you have developed a basis of trust with your friends and acquaintances, you can continue your campaigns with larger quantities and higher margins.[58]

Today you can take advantage of the services of specialized third party logistics providers. You don't have to check the quality of the goods yourself, you don't have to pack them yourself, and you don't have to ship them yourself. Modern service providers do all of these things competently and reliably and, above all, more cheaply than you could ever do it on your own. What has not been taken away from you is the puzzle, the idea, the concept, the design – and how you will exploit these possibilities.

You will certainly ask yourself: can I afford these experts? This is actually a question relating to the quality of your puzzle. If it's radical enough, if it's a disruptive innovation, and if it works with a high enough margin, you certainly can afford professional support. (The small independent businessman, on the other hand, who is doing what everyone else is doing and is exposed to tough competition, won't be able to afford our approach and method of operating.)

You're probably thinking it's cheaper to do things yourself rather than using third- party professional service providers. In practice, however, experience has often shown that if you take all of your own costs into account, you can buy such services more cheaply than what it would cost you to perform them yourself.

In summary, as unlikely as it may seem to you at the moment, you *can* "play with the big boys." But you should be prudent and limit yourself to supplying a single product or a single service. Marketing experts will try to talk you into diversification so that you can spread your risk. But be careful – you'll be paying for this with mushrooming complexity and higher unit costs. It was not without reason that Andrew Carnegie said, "Concentrate your energies, your thoughts and your capital.... The wise man puts all his eggs in one basket and watches the basket." The opportunity for you to become an expert in a single subject, keep track of your business and be superior to existing conventions in this one thing outweighs the risk of non-diversification.

Later, when you've gathered more experience and your concept has been successful in practice, you can expand, diversify or even bring the outsourced functions back into your company. At that point your risks will be manageable and calculable.

Today the belief that size and efficiency alone are sufficient has faded. Companies of a certain size are no longer agile enough for many processes. In contrast, attention is turning to small, flexible units. Today's entrepreneur doesn't need much more than a laptop and a cell phone.

> Anyone who has an idea
> doesn't need anything more than a kitchen table.
>
> JERRY AUERSWALD,
> German guitar maker,
> Maker of one-of-a-kind instruments for international stars.

7.8 Market Leader Overnight

www.myphotobook.de. For many years photo albums with lovingly selected memories delighted both young and old. They were close at hand and always on the shelf waiting for you. In contrast, the modern world of digital photography operates with USB sticks and folders on your computer. Goodbye photo album – or maybe not? Two young men from Berlin-Kreuzberg discovered it was possible to revive the idea of the photo album, but in contemporary form. You take your digital pictures, make a selection, e-mail them to myphotobook.de, and back comes a bound notebook or a book or a wallpaper mural, and all of a significantly higher quality than the photo albums of yesteryear.

What did they need to do this? Did founders David Diallo and Jan Christoph Gras invent or develop something new? Every child knows that you can use digital data to print and bind pictures. Do you need a high performance printer for this? Not necessarily, in any event not at the launch of the company. The same holds true for the bookbinding set-up.

But myphotobook.de adds yet another, completely different aspect to entrepreneurial design. It was a kind of super business model that gave it an extravagant launch in the market. This was because it provided many companies and their customers an additional benefit without their having to lift a finger.

The "normal" situation for start-up founders runs along these lines: you start a company, no one knows you, and probably no one has been waiting for you either. Now you have to draw attention to yourself. You're starting from zero and slowly work your way up to a profitable order of magnitude. myphotobook.de was different. Instead of opening a shop in Kreuzberg and maybe later expanding to Schöneberg, the founders thought about what company in the area of photo developing had the most customers. They determined that it wasn't a photo chain, but the drugstore Schlecker who was the market leader for digital photos. The founders contacted Schlecker and presented their proposal – that Schlecker offer its customers a *Schlecker photo album*. How would that work? You don't have to worry about that – we'll handle everything for you behind the scenes. This gave Schlecker an attractive new product to offer its customers, but freed it of all the organizational tasks needed to provide this benefit.

The advantage for myphotobook.de was that the young entrepreneurs became market leaders in Germany overnight and that they had a white label model they could offer to others in the photo business. But not only they – any other company or website could also offer their customers photo albums, for example, the German TV channel, "Pro7-Photobook." myphotobook.de became the market leader in Europe, held in high esteem in expert circles.

What components do you need to do this? A high-output printer and a binder for the loose pages. Machinery for production like this can be leased; it probably doesn't pay to buy this equipment at the beginning. This is certainly not the only example demonstrating that you can practice virtuoso entrepreneurship by applying pre-existing technology. What is special about it is the coordination needed to create a highly interesting entrepreneurial concept out of pre-existing components. Schumpeter observed long ago that many innovations that we sooner or later comprehend with surprise or amazement have long been in existence. Only a tiny fraction is really new. Most are a recombination of existing ideas and products.

Concepts like www.myphotobook.de have a turbo effect. The company www.spreadshirt.com administers more than 1,000 mini shops in which mini entrepreneurs create and sell their own sweatshirts. Anyone can open her or his own shop and get a share of the sales proceeds from the printed T-shirts. Today there are more than 200,000 shop partners.

7.9 A Company to Get in on – the Story of the CO_2 Campaign

A few years ago, we offered the following challenge to our customers:

You're not yet ready to put together your own company made up of components? That's OK. We'll take another step together and create a company for which all of the components have already been assembled. A ready-made company.

And this is what it looks like.

The Projektwerkstatt company has launched a CO_2 Campaign. The simplest and fastest way to save energy and do something to prevent climate change is through energy-saving light bulbs. Energy-saving bulbs are today's alternative to the technically obsolete incandescent bulb. The classic *incandescent bulb converts at most 5% of the energy consumed into light – the rest is wasted as heat. So now the objective is to make high quality energy-saving bulbs cheap. Applying the Tea Campaign principles – only one product, only economy-sized packages, no middleman and direct sales.*

And what does this have to do with you?
You can take advantage of the CO_2 Campaign's framework, that is, the processes for ordering, accounting and shipping logistics. This means you'll be handing over all the business administration tasks. And in so doing, you'll also be passing on all the problems of quality control, financing and the risk of whether you'll actually be able to sell all the goods you've purchased. For all practical purposes the Project Workshop will provide you with a virtual company. Free.

Why was the Projektwerkstatt doing this? Because it wants to trigger a revolution in entrepreneurship. Because I wanted then, and still want (as in this book), to demonstrate that entrepreneurial thinking and action don't have anything to do with bookkeeping, grueling management tasks and 12-hour days, and instead show that by using components and the division of labor it's possible to concentrate on essential tasks and questions like, "Where can I find really good products?" "How can I ship them as cheaply as possible to the end consumer – and without any delay?" and "What can I contribute to make the economy more transparent, effective and responsible?"

Participants were getting a company in minimalist form. A virtual, but fully functional company. Assembled almost entirely from components. If you joined up, you could focus on the essential task – making your little company successful by providing the world with something valuable, namely, useful and economical energy-saving light bulbs. Wasn't the Projektwerkstatt Company already doing this, though? Yes, but with your help it would be able to reach more people than it could on its own. Did this mean that you'd be only a salesperson? Well, that was not a bad thing if you could offer an intelligent product cheaper than the customary market price.

About 500 of our customers joined up to start their own little companies to participate in the CO_2 Campaign.

The CO_2 Campaign showed that it actually is possible to pursue entrepreneurship in such a way that you can delegate to the professionals all those business administration activities that are burdensome and require expertise. This allows you to move to the next step, to start composing your own company making use of components. Replace "CO_2 Campaign" with something else, something that seems to you reasonable and worth pursuing. The goal here is that you recognize that you can use an online shop as the framework for the *administration* of your own little independent company. The online shop will accomplish this. If you handle all your activities through a shop – *i.e.*, even your own orders that you want to use to supply your family, friends and neighbors directly – then you'll no longer need a bookkeeper since the shop will take over all the administrative duties for your little business.

But remember: it's not enough just to set up a shop and put in a product. You *do* have to think of something special. Otherwise not a soul will buy from you. Online shops are already a dime a dozen. This means you'll have to work on your concept. It's your brainpower that will determine how successful your little business will be.

7.10 Create a Company – While Keeping Your Day Job

As you've been reading this, you've probably already started asking yourself the question, "Do I have to give up my current job in order to be an entrepreneur?"

The answer given by most conventional business consultants is an unequivocal "Yes." By the time of the implementation stage at the latest, you'd be under enormous stress – the notorious 12-hour day – which consumes a founder's total time and energy.

But how would it be if you worked with professional components? Let's look at the situation a little more closely. A good idea concept, as we already know, does not spring into being overnight, nor does it arise without effort. It demands very intensive work, but of a kind that is not easily measured in hours or that must necessarily be performed sitting at a desk. Working on your own concept is not subject to the normal work rhythms of your regular job. Every individual has a unique working style, and we all analyze, research and create in our own way.

After years of working in a permanent job, many people have to figure out what approach suits them best when there's no longer a boss telling them what to do and how to do it. Even many of my students quickly fall into conventional patterns. Remember, what is necessary is to focus on function, not follow convention.

As is the case in the arts, good concepts require a certain amount of leisure for them to be able to emerge. We can't force these results in the way we can turn out work under the pressure of a deadline. Good things take time. Once we have set our mind on puzzling out a solution, many things that we otherwise would have ignored will fall into place by themselves. Like sudden tips from friends and colleagues who know about your plan. Things do fall into composition.

Once you have the concept, you go on to researching and identifying appropriate components. This, too, doesn't have to become a full-time job. Don't be satisfied with the first supplier to come along, just because you're happy to have found a component. Inquire, research, investigate, compare. Finally, you are ready to coordinate the components. This, too, is a manageable task where concepts are simple and straightforward.

Under these conditions – illustrated in the examples described above – founding a company can actually be a kind of part-time job. Launching a company with a safety net, so to speak. Don't give up your day job, your old occupation, until your own idea concept proves to be sound and sustainable. Wait for your *concept to prove itself*. Don't put all your money on one card, but establish your business on a carefully considered and securely solid basis. It is not true that the fast devour the slow in every situation, but those who are well-prepared and work with professional partners will succeed over those who are excitable, overworked and try to organize everything in-house.

8 How to Work Out Your Own High-Potential Concept: the Entrepreneurship Laboratory

Up until now little attention has been given to the systematic thought processes that must take place before launching a company. The focus of attention has not been on drafting, developing and refining the idea concept as an essential prerequisite for success. I find this amazing because entrepreneurs and their investors make a long-term commitment of time and capital. Therefore, attempting to reduce the risk through a systematic and effective process of entrepreneurial design serves an important function.

Our goal in the development of an entrepreneurial design must be to increase the probability of success by ensuring that the idea concept stands on more than one leg.

The little Laboratory man as the symbol of good Entrepreneurial Design:

He should be well-balanced and able to stand on more than one leg

This figure, which I use in my presentations, is intended to illustrate that entrepreneurial design contains aspects of both art and construction. The arrangement must be balanced in such a way that it has the flexibility to absorb external impacts and then return to a stable state.

In the market it is possible that competitors will introduce new advantages and that the founder's original market advantage will evaporate. Just when a concept functions well or a new technology is "in the air," it's common that a competitor offers a better price, higher quality or some other market advantage. Thus, if it is at all possible, a good entrepreneurial design should stand on more than one leg to survive such an external impact.

The little sculpture I use to demonstrate this idea can find a stable, balanced position on each of the four legs of the chair. In my own experience with the Tea Campaign, the real mainstay was a price significantly lower than what was charged by the competition. But if anyone had undercut our prices, we still would have had our other legs to rest on: the frequency and transparency of the chemical residue analyses; the guarantee that our tea was 100% Darjeeling; the Tea Campaign's efficient logistics (as a result of the simplicity of its concept), as well as our fair trade practices.

For many years the process of refining ideas has been the focal point of my Entrepreneurship Laboratory, a seminar for students and start-up founders who are already well along in their thought process toward launching a business. The Laboratory is a method to develop an initial idea into a mature and well-thought-out entrepreneurial design. The word "Laboratory," borrowed from the realm of the natural sciences, was consciously chosen to illustrate that this is a *systematic* process.

Participants are encouraged to stick with the system: Don't get off track. Work on the issues and sightlines, one after the other. Don't confuse this technique with "best practice"; that's a different method. Please keep Chapter 4.2 in mind. It is not about copying others. You have to work out a clearly identifiable market advantage over your established competitors. If you start by studying what the competition is doing, you will be easily ensnared by their model. You should be working on "next practice" rather than taking over someone else's "best practice."

8.1 Opening Up the Idea

In Germany, in a meeting with a conventional start-up adviser, the would-be founder brings the idea; the idea, so to speak, is simply "there." In the Laboratory, on the other hand, the idea is questioned, examined, refined. Like a sculptor, a founder can work the raw material and create an intellectual abstraction that reflects not only the concerns of the "artist" more clearly and more precisely, but that also develops a better view of the market. It is important to work out something that's "a better fit," something that dovetails with the personality of the founder, something that "feels" better to him or her than the initial idea.

In each case, we try to figure out what will truly engage the participant over the long term: what reflects his inclinations and desires, even those desires of which he might not be fully conscious. The method is akin to Frithjof Bergmann's concept of New Work, where the question posed is: "What do we really, really want?" Thus the goal is not simply to accept the idea and then address possible steps to implement it, but rather to treat the initial idea as the raw material whose potential still needs to be explored.

> Our desires
> are intimations of the capabilities
> that lie within us.
> They are the heralds of what
> we will be able to achieve.
>
> JOHANN WOLFGANG VON GOETHE

In this sense, the initial idea is only a heading, a first indication of where we can start looking for the ingredients that should ultimately yield an idea concept. I regard it as the modeling clay out of which you can create many forms. Accordingly, it is not uncommon that the discussion with the prospective founder takes a turn which that person does not expect. Although she is often convinced that she is at the end of the idea process and is already thinking about its implementation, I try to get a feel for whether she herself has actually considered the perspectives that have opened up with her idea. Following such a discussion, it is not uncommon that the founder ends up with ideas totally different from those she originally came with. The job of a consultant is not to give answers, but to ask lots of questions, especially questions that open up new perspectives. The founder must find the answers for himself. It has to be *his own* intellectual baby, not an idea from the consultant or one triggered by the funding guidelines.

> In a world of constant change, good questions
> are the real scarcity.
>
> Bad questions assign blame,
> change living processes
> into black-and-white phenomena,
> cement things into clichés,
> belittle the complexity of the world.
>
> On the other hand, good questions open things up.
>
> MATTHIAS HORX

Starting a new restaurant is a textbook example I am fond of using. A potential founder comes with an idea: "I'd like to launch a restaurant featuring Egyptian cuisine." A conventional business consultant would then ask about everything that's important for *operating* a restaurant. For example, the competitive situation, or the founder's competence in the areas important for running a restaurant. Implementation will be the focus here – to open a restaurant, you need money for decorating the premises, for a decent bar, and for the kitchen. Thus the question of capital comes up relatively soon.

The next problems are finding a good location and suitable staff for the restaurant. Now the founder is preoccupied by three things – his capital requirements, finding a suitable location, and selecting the appropriate personnel. The idea of an Egyptian restaurant now plays only a secondary role. It can be anticipated that the concept of the restaurant, if realized, will at best consist of only a few specific interior design elements; perhaps the chairs will be reminiscent of a pharaoh's throne, or a few pictures of Luxor may hang on the walls.

In spite of what appeared to be appropriate planning, which considered a variety of aspects, there's still a high degree of risk in this type of start-up. A lot of capital is required, and much advance preparation is needed, all of which will require financing. In addition, there are high operating costs like rent, interest and personnel. Unless there are a lot of customers immediately, as well as over the long term, there's a danger that this start-up will end up the same way that many other restaurants have ended up in the past. As far as the likelihood of survival goes, it's like placing bets in a casino – in both cases, the chances of success are statistically low. I put all my money on Red 19 and fervently hope it wins. If my restaurant doesn't work out, then I'll lose all of my own money, my borrowed capital, and all my work will have been in vain. I call this *launching a business à la Roulette*. Not recommended.

8.1.1 Finding Out What Really Motivates the Founder

My methodology is different. I start with the initial idea and ask the would-be founder probing questions: "Why do you want to run a restaurant? Because you like to be with people? Because you like to cook? Because you want to run your own business? Because you have pleasant associations with Egypt? Because you are fascinated by Upper Egypt?" His answers give me an initial sense of why the founder came up with this idea at all. Depending on his answers, I follow up with more relevant questions. If, for example, his answer was, "I like to be with people," my next questions would be "What do you find attractive about that? What role would you like to play? In what situations do you feel most comfortable with people? What kind of people would you like to surround yourself with? Are you single? Married? What are your hobbies?" If the founder replies, "I am very interested in Egypt," I would continue with my questions, "What was it that attracted you? Was it the people, the culture, the history, the food, the climate, the exotic history surrounding the pyramids and the pharaohs?"

What's important to me is to find out what motivates the potential founder and what was behind her original idea. Certainly you can imagine that it's possible to follow up on each line of questioning with many more questions. Ultimately you'll have an initial framework that will be on a solid footing because it's based on the inclinations, talents, desires and passions of the person in question, an approach that can tap the hidden energies of that individual.

Nonetheless it is a relatively open framework, and it still needs many pieces of the puzzle in the form of information, contacts and assessments of the potentialities before we will have built a durable edifice that can stand up to the storms of changing fashion, imitators, established competitors and bureaucratic hurdles, as well as the many other obstacles, both expected and unexpected, that inevitably arise when you start a new venture.

Thus it is not an inspiration or a sudden epiphany that makes for a good entrepreneurial design. It is based on *systematic* work – the more, the better. Only when the entrepreneurial design addresses as many aspects as possible would I recommend a start-up. In my experience it is often the case that introspection or a closer examination into one's own as well as the customers' desires are more promising than chasing trends or opportunities.

> If you want to do something really interesting and revolutionary,
> learn to ignore your customers.
>
> Most customers function like rear view mirrors.
> They are extremely conservative and boring,
> lack imagination
> and don't know their own minds.
>
> RIDDERSTRÅLE & NORDSTRÖM
> in: *Funky Business: Talent makes capital dance*

The verdict is that it's much too fast to go from initial idea directly into business administration implementation. The potential created by working through the initial idea into a well-thought-out and mature entrepreneurial design should not be neglected.

8.1.2 Trying Out New Perspectives

I start the process in the Laboratory by asking questions; later on, members of the audience join in. Take Egypt, for example. What impressions are evoked by this name? A trip to Egypt? Can you imagine a totally different trip to Egypt? Perhaps a virtual trip? What do we know about Tutankhamen's daily life from archeological finds? Could you work with the local Egyptian museum? Can you imitate the life of the Pharaohs?

At this point, where archeologists are held back by their academic standards, you (as a travel agent, restaurant owner or event planner) are free to speculate wildly without fearing a negative impact on your career. Just like a filmmaker, you can create the pharaoh out of a mixture of science and fiction.

Here we see another advantage of entrepreneurship emerging. You can draw creatively from all kinds of areas, whether science, fantasy, movie props, literature, humor, or anything else.

I am often asked: how do you know when an entrepreneurial design is mature? And I say: you'll feel it in your gut. When you've developed a good design with clear market advantages, one that addresses possible imitators and their vulnerabilities and all the other things that a good design should achieve, when you've thought everything through and found the answers, then you won't be able to sit still any longer.

> Kick your brain
> and your ass will follow.
>
> (Modified from:
> Kick your ass, and your brain will follow.)

At this point you can't shake the anxiety that you might miss out on this opportunity if you don't get started immediately. You want to start running. And just as with a child who's ready to be born when the time has come, you'll want to introduce your entrepreneurial baby to the world. As long as you have doubts, don't launch a start-up! Take your doubts seriously; look for solutions.

I know my advice here is diametrically opposed to that of conventional business consultants. But my years of experience tell me that I am right. Too many failed start-ups. Too many half-baked ideas. Too much readiness to take on obligations that can't be worked off through commercial activity. High indebtedness and low conceptual potential – this is too little to work with.

Of course there are different paths to success besides developing a creative entrepreneurial design. Even a snack bar can be successful if it's located on the right corner. There are also profits to be had from a me-too idea that merely imitates, or from an import-export business taking advantage of the arbitrage effect. However, a more elegant route is through creativity. In a post-industrial society, land, capital, or labor become progressively less important as resources; what is becoming more important is creativity.

"How would the world look if I could ride on a beam of light?" – thus began Einstein's ponderings on the theory of relativity. He was 14 years old at the time. Encountering a problem, considering a variety of routes and choosing the most practical – this type of mental agility can be taught.

Does entrepreneurship demand exceptional and highly creative people? No. All of us occupy ourselves with more or less creative activities every day. Every child is creative as an artist. According to Picasso, what we must ask ourselves is how that child can remain an artist once s/he grows up. Not all people are equally creative, but in many instances, their original potential for reasoning and creating is underdeveloped, buried or blocked. Creativity is not a mystical, god-given talent, but a competence that can be systematically guided and taught.

In his play *Le bourgeois gentilhomme* the playwright Molière tells the story of a man who asks what prose is and to his astonishment learns that he has been speaking it all his life. The same holds true for creativity; half the people in the world believe it is a mysterious quality possessed by the other half of humanity.[59] However, many studies show that everyone is able to make use of his or her creativity.

8.2 Seven Techniques for Working Out an Entrepreneurial Design

> There are painters who make a yellow spot out of the sun. But there are others who through their artistry and intelligence make the sun out of a yellow spot.
>
> PABLO PICASSO

This book is not the place to describe techniques for improving one's creativity. There are hundreds of books on the subject with many useful recommendations; but please permit me a few remarks.

The American doctor, psychiatrist and author Frederick Flach points out that the creative act is not something that comes out of thin air; rather, it re-arranges already existing facts, ideas and systems, combining them with one another. The capacity for creativity in many people has become stunted, whether it's because the environment in which they grew up disapproved of creativity and originality, or because they were molded by a school system that promoted intellectual conformity, or because they worked in organizations that didn't permit any imagination in structuring their own activities. Another source of inhibition lies in the erroneous notion that you must have a unique talent for creativity. In contrast to this, Flach emphasizes that the ability to think and act creatively is a universal human strength. The author cites two important rules that I, too, have found to be reinforced again and again in my workshops. First, at the start you must postpone your own judgment, and second, quantity results in quality. Of course it goes against the grain to hold back criticisms during the search for ideas and simply to develop as many ideas as possible, especially ideas that might at the start seem unrealistic and illogical. But it is precisely these two rules that are important, because the ideas that come to us first are usually stereotypical and do not bring us as far along as the ideas that will come to us later. All of us have a tendency, both regarding our own ideas as well as the ideas of others, not to let them stand, but instead, after they have barely been articulated, to immediately analyze and criticize them. The arguments might indeed be very good ones, but they will block the development of new and better ideas.[60]

Anyone who studies creativity in depth will be confronted with a profusion of theories, methods and techniques.[61] Over the years I have worked out seven techniques for developing successful idea concepts. They are selected from an almost infinite number of techniques that are known, and in my opinion they are especially suitable for the subject of entrepreneurial idea development. I have tried to give them names that are as simple as possible, so please don't be put off by how elementary they sound. A technique is not made better by giving it a pretentious or cryptic name.

Commonly imitation and arbitrage[62], that is, the transfer of successful models that already exist in a region or other country, are two approaches that initially sound reasonable and were successful for a long time.

These days imitation and arbitrage are less suitable for start-ups. Why? Because information is no longer available only to you. It's public knowledge that's accessible to all. Generally others will be quicker than you are due to the instant dissemination of market prices, *e.g.*, on the Internet, or international trend scouts who are on the lookout for market opportunities for large companies, not to mention the big budgets that the major players invest in imitating successful business models. While you're still fiddling with your web page, a giant competitor with concentrated market strength may already be offering the product for sale. To be sure, you can attack the big guys, but not in the areas of arbitrage or imitation.[63]

8.2.1 Discover Potential in What Exists Already

Successful entrepreneurial designs are often innovative without inventing anything new. The innovation lies in recombination. Early on, Schumpeter drew a distinction between innovations and inventions. It often takes quite some time before great inventions are market-ready because they harbor minor defects that make them fail. This is because when they're first introduced, they haven't yet been perfected technically, their significance may not yet be recognized, or they haven't been accepted by the public. This is the reason why successful business people are generally not inventors but innovators. They rely on what already exists.

The American economist Israel M. Kirzner[64] emphasized this as well; he regarded "discovering what exists" as the entrepreneur's core business. This concept only appears to be a paradox. Something that already exists doesn't have to be re-invented, but its significance and potential can nonetheless be interpreted in a fresh way and re-discovered. A famous example of this is the fax machine. The invention has been around for a long time,[65] but ultimately it was introduced worldwide by companies other than the inventor or the companies that had initially tried to market it.

Skype is a good example of the Kirzner theorem built on Schumpeter's theory. Another example is Sergio Rial, the Brazilian bank manager who was sent to China to establish the ABN AMRO Bank there. He learned about the country's banking sector, but in the process he became aware of something totally unrelated – chicken feet. Yes, chicken feet, which are eaten in China. Not just the thighs and legs that we eat, but also the claws, which are regarded as a delicacy. What every other visitor to China had already seen, Rial viewed with more alert eyes. In Brazil nobody eats chicken feet. Nor do they eat them in Argentina and the other South American countries. And Brazil and Argentina are among the world's leading producers of chickens. What happens to the chicken feet there? They're thrown away. You can imagine how the story ends. You can read all about it in a brief report in the *Far Eastern Economic Review* – Rial started coordinating the stream of chicken feet going from South America to Asia. He discovered something that already existed and ensured that the chicken feet would be used well.

> The real discovery is not finding unknown territory,
> but seeing things with new eyes.
>
> MARCEL PROUST

8.2.2 Function, not Convention

Many of our examples demonstrate the entrepreneurs' independent spirit above all. They are either free from, or are able to shake off convention. Conversely, this means there is promise of success if I regard everything I find in place as convention, at least until the opposite has been proven. I examine the processes without being intimidated and ask myself whether those things that were still thought to be reasonable in the past can now be organized more simply using modern methods. I don't settle for making a service or product a little cheaper, better, more efficient, smarter or more environmentally friendly, but instead I challenge the entire process, that is, I start to fundamentally rethink how it would be possible to organize the functions under current conditions.

I described this process in detail using the Tea Campaign as my example. Holger Johnson's ebuero also falls into this category, as does Ingvar Kamprad's approach to rethinking the furniture business.

Years ago a major tea dealer, with a nod to his family's tradition, showed me a diagram – today we'd call it an organizational chart – of how the international tea business is structured, how he had learned the tea business during his apprenticeship. In his wildest dreams he would not have imagined that this could be altered so radically. He told me, "It was necessary to have someone like you, a total outsider, who could analyze the accustomed processes without any undue deference."

But in fact the technique is very easy. If you want to deal in a product, do *not* ask about the details, for example about the packaging, wrapping the pallets, retailers, wholesalers, importers, exporters or other marketing structures; simply ask yourself: how can I bring the product from its source to the customer, how can I organize the process as simply as possible and make use of components? So that the only thing that remains for me to do is to organize the components.

With this technique your chances are best if you're a newcomer to the field and not yet inhibited by occupational blinders. Function, not convention doesn't require a great deal of previous knowledge, only rigorous thinking and an objective disregard of what has come before.

If you are rigorous in your focus on function, then this question will arise on its own: what can you leave out? What in the conventional form is superfluous – and only costs money? Here I am not necessarily talking about giving something up. Quite the opposite. An entrepreneur's ambition should be for the best. If you don't have money, you must be creative.

Simplicity is a good principle. Complexity is the entrepreneur's enemy. If you believe that "paring down" and "simplicity" are too basic, not impressive enough, and not at all grand, then remember Leonardo da Vinci: "Simplicity is the ultimate perfection."

8.2.3 Recombining What Already Exists

The example that I find to be the most illustrative is the following :

"Think ceramic," says Thijs Nel, an artist in Magaliesberg near Johannesburg. His art form is ceramics. Confronted with the slums in his vicinity, he got an idea for how to build better houses. Traditionally the residents of this South African township built their homes out of mud, with the walls reinforced with stakes and branches. However, when the termites eat the wood, they create excellent channels for water, and the houses don't last long in rainy weather.[66]

You could describe Nel's entrepreneurial idea as follows: Imagine a cup. Turn the cup upside down. Make the cup bigger and bigger in your mind's eye. Now imagine holes in this cup. Now let's call this cup a "house."

Now like other ceramic wares, this house-sized cup with holes as windows must be fired at a high temperature. The firing can be organized with the help of other villagers. The result is a house that's much more durable than traditional huts, but hardly more expensive.

The artist as architect and entrepreneur, with an idea, astoundingly simple and demonstrably practical. Everyone can be his own builder, potter, and artist. It's even highly likely that the townships will be more attractive than the accomplishments of many trained architects.

Now you may say, that's nothing new. Many peoples, such as the Hopi Indians, built in this manner. That's right, Nel also didn't discover anything new, but looked for an inexpensive. traditional material for his cup idea, a material you could find everywhere – and he combined something familiar in a new way. A technique as simple as it is effective – which you can also come up with through systematic thinking.

8.2.4 Fulfilling More Than One Function

In modern societies characterized by a division of labor, more and more functions are separated from others. This means that to eat, we go to a restaurant. There are youth clubs for young people and senior clubs for the seniors. Every function has its own space. To buy things you have to go to a store. You borrow books in the library and go to the office to work. Plays are presented in the theater; audacious directors bring extravagant productions – where? To the stage, in a theater.

The isolation and loneliness that exist in modern societies are related to this division of labor. Everyone is sitting in his or her own space. Why are we so delighted by the tiny French villages we know from our vacations? Young and old sit together; some read, others play cards, and somewhere in the midst of this a barber is cutting somebody's hair. In many places our work world is so streamlined and so differentiated that it offers us the opportunity to reintegrate functions.

Many years ago I held a workshop on the subject of business hours where without any preconceived ideas the participants examined multiple uses for buildings. What events could you hold in a supermarket? Why isn't a law office used for exhibitions during the day and as party space at night? How can you make use of space that is unused part of the time? Perhaps a bed store as a place to test-drive a mattress overnight, or maybe even as an unconventional hotel?

Being able to serve more than one function has significant economic advantages. You don't have to build, furnish, illuminate and heat these spaces. The only limits are set by your own imagination.

Reintegration brings not only economic advantages, but it also serves a good societal function. It counteracts isolation; it brings people together who would otherwise have little to do with one another.

We can learn from nature, which uses things many times over. It is rare that something has only one function. From the biologists and ecologists we learn that a blade of grass fulfills at least six functions. Applying this notion to an entrepreneurial idea, you should be asking yourself: what things are piling up in some place that I can utilize for free somewhere else? What I'm talking about isn't waste recovery, but a good eye for things that were devised for other processes, which I can reuse for my own purposes for as low an investment as possible. In nature, multiple uses are the norm, and highly diverse forms of cooperation have developed which have made mutual economic uses possible.

During my student years I often didn't have an apartment of my own; instead, I moved into friends' apartments as a room sitter. Not only did this provide me with variety, but it was also very luxurious. I didn't have to set up housekeeping or pay for it, and I got acquainted with books, art and objects of everyday use from all over the world that I would never have encountered in my own apartment. And my hosts were happy, too, because I was careful with their things, watered their plants and at the end gave them a generous gift. A present that cost only a fraction of what I would have had to have paid in rent. Luxurious also because I did not have to deal with landlords and gas and electric bills, bureaucratic things that all of us dislike.

For a long time I lived out of a suitcase and later made an entire move in a VW Beetle with a sunroof. It is similar to hitchhiking: before I had my own car, I met lots of people, and every day was a great adventure. Later I drove my own car, and from then on I had to worry about repairs, taxes, and insurance bills. Every unfamiliar engine sound could be an ominous sign that some repair would soon be needed. This is not even primarily about money, but about effort and loss of focus, about complexity. The focal point of my ideas is how to do the most with the least effort. I'm not speaking in favor of freeloading, but of intelligent combinations that create a win-win situation for everyone.

8.2.5 Seeing Problems as Opportunities

Problems are a wonderful hook to develop ideas for their solution. For beginners: while most people are annoyed when it starts to rain, the entrepreneur says: now is the best time to sell umbrellas. For the more advanced: when the Berlin Wall fell, there emerged what we called "wallpeckers," people who tried to hammer souvenirs for themselves out of the concrete. Most hammers weren't up to the task. What did you really need? A chisel. You could make a bundle selling chisels.

Or take the example of the water hyacinth. In tropical climates it's an invasive plant, a plague that flourishes in rivers and lakes, multiplies quickly and clogs the waters, causing great damage. For natives and tourists alike it's an everyday sight. But it's also a material that's readily available. The raw material is simply there; you don't have to plant it, fertilize it or fence it in. You simply harvest it – and do something useful with it.

A lot of thought, even supported by the UN, was given to how you could turn the water hyacinth into something useful. Theoretically you could use it as feed for pigs and for compost, but with a 98% water content and the rest a tough fiber, it was not economically useful, even for most other uses. Research on this plant, without practical results, could fill a thick volume.

Impressed by the silky sheen of the plant stems when forced through the rotating cylinders of a mangle, one designer began to work with the material. Woven artistically around a rattan frame, the dried stems can be used to make chairs that are both attractive and sturdy. For the designer, an interesting variation in material. But what does this mean for an economist? Not much if he focuses on the conventional questions asked in his field. Is there a growth market here? No. Perhaps a market niche where you can get started without much competition? Not really.

This is what makes the difference between the entrepreneur and the traditional economist. He recognizes the potential in something despite the fact that it doesn't fit the recognized economic paradigm. Water hyacinths? No potential. Studied extensively but with no result. Chairs? The furniture market is already saturated.

It was only by chance that I became aware of the chair. The lovely piece was in the studio of the Thai designer Khun Tük. Neither part, the water hyacinth or the chair, was by itself particularly promising. Seen together, the two materials are a provocation – a weed becomes a raw material of unlimited potential.

Presented in this way, the water hyacinth could give rise to the impression that problems more or less solve themselves. This impression would be incorrect. Years passed between the initial idea, research and experimentation and finally the mature idea. It took another three years from the first prototype to the sales launch of water hyacinth chairs in Germany. In the meantime a little industry has grown out of this in Thailand.

8.2.6 Turning Work into Fun and Entertainment

You remember the tale of Tom Sawyer, the hero of Mark Twain's 1876 novel. One day Tom is forced to paint the fence around Aunt Polly's house – and of all days, on a beautiful Saturday when all his friends are going swimming and sunning themselves.

When his first friend saunters by, Tom isn't spared his sarcasm. But our hero keeps his head. Who would want to swim if he had the chance to paint a fence? Tom plunges himself into the work with enthusiasm, daubs a little paint here, studies a not yet perfectly painted spot there. His friend Ben gets curious, and wonders whether he'd be allowed to paint a little too.

By the end of the day Tom has convinced his friends that it's exciting to paint a fence. But even better, they pay him for allowing them to do the work. *Turning work into fun.*

Can this little tale be transferred to entrepreneurial design? I think so; Tom managed to organize the job of painting a fence in a very special way. With a little imagination and talent for organization, Tom understood that you can turn even a punishment into a party.

Examples of designs like this are easy to imagine – a pub where the guests draft the beer, or vacations-on-the-farm where the visitors can milk a cow. For the farmer's wife who has to milk many cows every day, it's hard work, but for the visitor it's an adventure. If I intended to become a farmer, I'd try to radically rethink "farm." What animals are appropriate? What crops? How would you make sure that your visitors met and made friends with each other? What activities, celebrations or transformations will take place? What can you do to ensure your visitors will come back? What activities can the visitors take over in the long run? Don't start thinking about what's already happening, *e.g.*, picking your own strawberries. Approach it systematically. Not everything has to remain hard work; it can also be fun. It's helpful if in your mind's eye you can break down repetitive tasks into small manageable segments and make sure that there is variety. Even the old Romans knew that "*Variatio delectat*!"

8.2.7 Turning Visions into Reality

Unfortunately, not all visionaries get to see their ideas transformed into successful companies during their own lifetime. But some do. Perhaps the most famous anecdote is the tale of a young man who for 18 long years tried to get a horse coach to propel itself forward in a controlled manner, using the power from the combustion of gasoline. He suffered one failure after another. His father thought his notion of seating people on an explosive device was dangerous and irresponsible; his friends and acquaintances thought he was incompetent, even crazy. They had proof of this when our innovator wanted to drive his vehicle out of the barn. It turned out that his coach was larger than the barn door, and a wall had to be torn down to get it out.

In 1903 he took part in an auto race, and reached the finish line, which at that time could not be taken for granted. Only from that point on did people start paying attention to him. The name of our hero? Henry Ford. His ineffectual beginnings are missing from the books written about him later, and even from his own autobiography. Turning visions into reality is a technique for advanced adventurers, or for very goal-oriented people, but on a small scale, it applies to many founders.

Those were the seven techniques, and while not every technique is appropriate for every entrepreneurial design, it is worthwhile to approach your model from as many different perspectives as possible. Don't be too quick to say you are almost finished, because every model becomes better when you take advantage of more perspectives.

In my workshops I make sure the participants come from a variety of different fields so they can draw upon a wide spectrum of ideas and perspectives. It's helpful to invite people who have already been engaged in social or political issues because they can put their finger on conditions that could be improved. With them you feel their energy, you feel that they really want to change things. It's not uncommon that such participants, who want to make a difference, don't want to wait any longer for large organizations like political parties or interest groups, but recognize entrepreneurship as the appropriate vehicle to put their ideas into practice, faster and with more focus, and in the process even to open up economic perspectives for their own lives.

8.3 The Sense and Nonsense of Business Plans

Now that it's been over a decade since my friend Sven Ripsas started the first Business Plan Competition in Germany, it's time to take stock. As it turns out, the results are quite mixed. An empirical study in the summer of 2005 asked all the winners of the Berlin Business Plan Competition from 1996 through 2004 about their business plans and the realization of these plans.[67]

One thing that stands out immediately: looking back, many of those surveyed warn against a misguided belief in the business plan that founders these days must develop for the Business Administration office, banks, or to apply for start-up grants. It appears it wasn't made sufficiently clear during the competition that the business plan is actually less relevant than the process by which sound entrepreneurial design is ideally conceived. The recognition that the business plan by itself isn't of such great value isn't new in the international arena, but this insight does seem to have been lost over time. Jeffry Timmons, one of the pioneers of business-plan-based start-ups, and one of the field's most prominent authors, stated very clearly that the written document should not be elevated to a mantra;[68] in principle, he said, a business plan is already out of date the minutes it emerges from the printer.[69]

Many highly successful businesses were launched without a formal business plan, and this isn't very surprising. The value of a business plan, such as it is, lies in the thought processes that were set in motion. The effort to understand the market and, in the process, to conceive better products and a more efficient entrepreneurial design, is what's decisive.

But good intentions can easily turn into the opposite of what's intended, as the filling out of templates and the answering of questions found in every chapter of the competition guidelines requires a kind of mechanistic mindlessness among the would-be founders. Instead of working out one's own idea concept, they are asked to generate very precise answers to individual questions. Another problem is that by linking funding to the steps presented in the plan, attention to unforeseen market signals is limited and too little room is left for spontaneous learning.

The three-year projections presented in the business plan are yet another story. Start-up entrepreneurs are supposed to make assumptions about how sales, profits and financing will develop over a three-year period. A requirement like this sounds more reasonable than it actually is.

Imagine you're supposed to forecast minute 57 of a soccer game. Total nonsense, you say? Then consider the following. A soccer game takes place in a relatively simple and stable environment. The playing field is clearly defined. Both sides have eleven players. The rules of the game are known in advance and do not change in the course of the game. By contrast, what does the environment look like in which a start-up operates? The playing field *is not clearly defined*. It has an ill-defined connection with parallel playing fields, where similar products compete with your own, even if not directly. (Consider the cell phone market. There you are in direct competition with other cell phone providers, while you are in indirect competition with "adjoining playing fields" like Skype, Google Talk and of course the old land line system.) And what about the number of players? The answer is that their number is constantly changing. Whole new teams are added during the game, new start-ups as well as established players with new products. Some give up during the game and disappear. Even the rules of the game change. A big discounter enters the market, someone offers your product or your service on the Internet, or a technological advance suddenly changes both the products and the market.

Thus, you could argue, it would be much easier to predict the stages of a soccer game than the various situations a start-up might encounter, and that over the much longer period of three years. Why then cling to projections? The obligation to make such calculations, we are told, encourages thinking in scenarios, and that's helpful. Maybe so; however, 70% of all market assumptions in business plans turn out to be wrong.[70] Economists are aware that when it comes to the market, they are always operating with incomplete information.

According to Ripsas, who brought the idea back from Babson College in Massachusetts, the value of business plans is overestimated in Germany. The 2005 study mentioned above showed that five years down the road, even the winners of the Business Plan Competition don't deliver above average performance in the market.[71]

What, then, is left of the business plan? A rite of passage perhaps, required to gain access to bank loans– if you really need them. For investors, it seems to be more a form of insurance in the event that something goes wrong and the start-up develops in a totally different way than was mapped out in the three-year plan. Then it can be said, in defense, that due diligence was followed and that the business plan had looked very persuasive.

8.4 ... and How Can I Draw Attention to my Start-Up?

8.4.1 Going from Zero to One

Nobody knows you. Nobody has been waiting for you. To get from zero to one you need a mathematical factor of infinity. Quite demanding. In contrast: to go from one to ten is only a factor of ten. So the difficult stage is really the beginning. How can I draw attention to my company?

Forget about conventional marketing. Marketing, too, can be envisioned as putting the pieces of a puzzle together, but you don't have to pursue an extravagant, expensive marketing plan. After all, we want to make our products reasonably priced and not throw away money on marketing. But what is important here is to forget the word "marketing" because it evokes false ideas. Instead, let's just call it, "How do I attract attention to my cause?" What is the message I want to convey? *What am I shooting for?* What can I use to make my mission known?

> *Shoot for the moon.*
>
> *Even if you miss,*
> *you'll land among the stars.*
>
> LES CHARM
> Babson College

Use your head, not your pocketbook. The task of getting attention can also be approached as creating a masterpiece of ideas.

As we've argued, the heart and soul of your company is the idea concept. That's where you already have an advantage that distinguishes you from the other, conventional start-ups. Your advantage is that you can promote an idea, not just some product. You have a cause, you're committed to an idea and you have to win your potential customers for this idea. In this situation, don't make the mistake of falling back on conventional marketing. You shouldn't make your pitch through putting advertisements in the newspaper, crafting ad placement campaigns or arranging for commercials. Before you listen to a so-called marketing expert and consider all the conventional advertising media mentioned above, ask yourself a few questions. What's persuasive about my idea? What means can I use to illustrate it? Precisely because you've developed your own concept, because you've created something new, you mustn't resort to conventional methods. You could say that each idea requires very specific, very individual methods to fit it.

Take for example Xing and studiVZ.[72] How did they, in a field with many newly launched social networks, manage to become the two most successful social networks in Germany?

In an interview with Lars Hinrichs, Xing's founder, he describes how the question of how to bring people together better had been on his mind for many years. How you could make it easier for them to get into contact with one another. How to create an occasion, and what kind of information could be helpful to do so. According to Hinrichs, it was these elements that made the breakthrough possible.

Ehssan Dariani, who launched studiVZ, bet on his own unique way to stimulate interest. "*Gruscheln*" – a word he coined – is a kind of Internet pick-up. Contemporaries mock the word "*Gruscheln*," a composite made up of *grüßen* – to greet – and *kuscheln* – to snuggle (in whatever way this may materialize over the Internet). He was sharply criticized in the media for a number of other provocative actions. Dariani himself calls this "*Radau* Marketing," which could perhaps be roughly translated as "in-your-face marketing." Around June 2006, the network enjoyed dynamic growth, in a little bit more than a month becoming the market leader among comparable services for students.

What interests us on the side is how significant these founders thought knowledge of business administration was. Even after being asked, both founders had little to say about this. Sure, you had to keep good books. Sure, expenses couldn't exceed your resources. Don't hire dilettantes for those jobs, thank you very much. But keep your brain available for more essential questions. And in both examples they weren't business administration questions, but rather involved social imagination, stages of experimentation and the belief in the practicability of their own, well-conceived concepts. A good concept is the best marketing tool.

As in the case of Duttweiler or Roddick, the economic result is a "byproduct" of the ideas. Profit orientation, business administration and management do not stand in the foreground, but one's own concept does, combined with an instinct for trends and deep personal commitment. Today Xing's value on the stock exchange is set at nine figures, and the price Holzbrinck Verlag paid for StudiVZ was not much lower. These aren't wishful-thinking valuation figures from the time of the first Internet boom, but plausibly objective assessments of the value of extensive networks and their use potential, including their economic potential.

8.4.2 We Are the Brands

Does it say in the economists' Bible that marketing expenses always have to get bigger? "How long," Seth Godin asks, "are we going to have to buy products for big money when we know very well that they're produced for a fraction of the price?" While the marketing experts tried to convince me that brands were becoming more and more important and that I had to invest much more money into the "Tea Campaign" brand, I was thinking in a totally different direction.

It would make sense to me if companies said, "we're investing enormous amounts in the quality of our products and are keeping the price as low as possible." I'd be happy to buy products like that, and I'd urge my friends and acquaintances to do the same. In reality something different is happening. Today, creating and "nurturing" a brand and drawing the public's attention to it swallows up significantly more money that the cost of the product itself.[73] In the past I liked the products of a well-known company with a color in its name; its products were regarded as especially durable and attractively designed. After my electric razor and toothbrush kept wearing out at ever-shorter intervals, even though the company was more profitable than ever, I started to have my doubts.

Protect intellectual property? Yes. But allow ourselves to be lulled in by brand names, while having to pay for this out of our own pockets? No. Is talking about frugality, simplicity and personal initiative a relapse into bourgeois-conservative patterns? Is criticism of brands and their efforts to manipulate us hopelessly out-of-date, just leftover anti-capitalist rhetoric? I don't think so. On the contrary. There is a reasonable chance that we can "take back" a part of the economy and make it our own, that we can score points in the competition of ideas and concepts.

We need to show how the new perspectives opened up by entrepreneurship enable broad and active participation in the economy. Not just on some abstract, theoretical level, but with practical examples that the rest of us can emulate. It would be a shame if we were to leave these opportunities to the still elatively small number of business founders and their investors who occupy the playing field today.

Even in the field of fashion, I can imagine devising our own "brands," custom-tailored to ourselves. In part, this is because I'd like to be a brand of my own, instead of being forced to purchase my image, respectability or attractiveness by means of expensive watches and exclusive brand name trousers and shirts. The other reason is that I had the good fortune to meet Professor Kambartel, at one time a professor of philosophy at the University of Constance.

Kambartel always wore the same light-colored trousers and a practical shirt equipped with many pockets. He explained that he didn't want to spend his limited time on earth on something as silly as poking around in the men's department of a department store. If he found something he liked, then on his next visit it wouldn't be there anymore. So he had decided to buy multiples of an item all at once, instead of starting over again every time he had a need for clothes.

I know considerations like this still sound strange to many people. Anyone who wants to while away his free time will feel right at home in boutiques and clothing stores. But what about the people who don't want to spend their time this way, but instead would rather occupy themselves with things that are important to them and who have the good fortune to be able to make this their profession? They're happy there are companies that maintain their product line unchanged over the long term. My assistant Barbara is an example. She always buys her lipstick from the same company because, for the past 15 years at least, this company has been making the same color, which is the one that looks most becoming on her. The lipstick has not gotten more expensive; nonetheless it's surely not unprofitable for the company if it's able to avoid frequent changes in its product line. Appropriately, the name of the lipstick is "Be Yourself."

Back to Professor Kambartel. First, I would like to stress that despite the sameness of his trousers and shirts, he was very popular with his students. His appeal came from his being different; he lived according to what made sense to him as a philosopher. And this resonated with his students, not because he was a professor, but because he was authentic.

Let's create an entrepreneurial idea from this. You bring your favorite trousers, your favorite shirt or your favorite blouse to "Kambartel," the company that creates charm through authenticity. Trousers, shirt and blouse are made for you in quantity, let's say 20 pieces at a time. You choose a good fabric, one that doesn't get baggy after five runs through the washing machine and doesn't stain the rest of your wash. Someone has carefully selected good quality fabric for you, and made it available at a reasonable price because it was bought in bulk. Catalogs aren't necessary because you, not the producer, are the one who is proposing the product. Shipping costs per item are also not significant. The company is not risking anything because it is making these items to order and not, as is customary in the fashion industry, putting something on the market, which one hopes will be bought, but which is expensive because the manufacturer knows that a portion will not be sold, and this must be factored into the original price.

Not a bad idea. "Kambartel" is a company with a genuine message instead of an artificial mission statement, which by now has almost become mandatory in the business world.[74] The risks are minimal, as are the capital outlays, since everything will be paid for in advance. Moreover, the level of expertise required is within reasonable limits, since naturally we will be working with components for the fabric selection, manufacturing and shipping logistics. Brand cultivation, which represents a major share of the costs of stylish clothing, has been completely eliminated. We can choose whether we will have our products made in Düsseldorf, Hong Kong, Capetown, Dakar or Lima. Even goods made in Germany can be cheaper than comparable items sold in department stores because you will save many of the customary expenses.

Remember also that the conventional means of bringing something to market is extremely expensive. On the conventional playing field you don't have a chance. You simply don't have the financial means (and even if you did have sufficient capital, you should be spending it in a better place). Classical advertising media are available to large, established companies, but not to you as a start-up founder. It is fruitless for you to enter into a battle of resources with established competitors. You have wonderful opportunities to attack large competitors, but not in a battle of resources. As in the story of David and Goliath, you have to use your brains, your creativity and your wits, not the raw power of the giants.

8.4.3 Flaunting Your Idea ...

You can also approach marketing by way of flaunting your idea, of staging it extravagantly. . There's no limit to our imagination. May I offer some examples?

ebuero offers attractive prices for office services. But don't you need professional marketing, considering the number of other providers already on the market? How do you make people sit up and take notice that you have revolutionized the way to run an office? What if you're a student, 22 years old, without much capital?

Holger Johnson filled one entire floor of an old factory building (which needed new flooring anyway) with 16 tons of Caribbean sand, then added palm trees, a bar, boccia balls and Frisbees. Now the office was a beach. Barefoot, in a dark suit, he sat down on an empty tea crate to have his picture taken. It was this story, with this picture, that got more than 60 German media outlets to write about the new company. You wouldn't be able to pay for an advertising campaign like this! (By the way, the sand cost less than a new floor.)

One day in December I ran into a man making his way down the street dressed as a Christmas tree with lights. Baffled, I stopped and looked. Children were pointing at him, shoppers carrying Christmas gifts turned to look at him. I followed along a few steps behind him, then congratulated him on his costume and asked about his motive. Grinning, he told me, "I sell candles – since I got this costume, I really stand out." I invited him to the university so that I could get my students to come up with their own ideas instead of putting their trust in marketing textbooks. He actually showed up, with a TV crew close on his heels. They only wanted

Holger Johnson, founder of ebuero

pictures of him; they paid no attention to me. Instant stardom!

If there were an Oscar for self-promotion, you'd have to award it to Karl Lagerfeld. He understood how to establish himself in the public consciousness through minor breaches of convention. When he began wearing a ponytail, it was virtually unthinkable for a man to get himself up in such a feminine way. Even "worse," – and to this day still all but unique – he fanned himself with a hand-held Japanese fan. In my classes I regularly ask my students what makes Karl Lagerfeld's fashions special. No one can say, but they all know Karl Lagerfeld. It seems you can establish a brand known the world over through minor breaches of convention that harm no one but take the viewer by surprise. As for the economics of the thing: it can't cost much to put your hair in a ponytail, and the fan set him back 5 Euros at the most. Remarkably efficient, given the attention it produced.

There is something else about this story. Imagine that we engage an ad agency to conduct a survey about Karl Lagerfeld. What do people think about the fashion czar? Every time my own little surveys of my students yield one unambiguous conclusion: "Well, that business with the ponytail is pretty strange. And then that fan, too – far out. Good grief. He really should stop that ." And imagine if we acted on the result of the survey. The customer is king, right? Lagerfeld without his ponytail and fan. How would that work? Lagerfeld is successful precisely because he is *not* following marketing surveys. His self-created authenticity is the reason he became a brand.

What is the common thread throughout these examples? The appetite for self-staging always plays a significant role. There is an element of playfulness that the candle salesman had to act on, just as Holger Johnson did for his ebuero. The more original your concept, the easier it is for you to produce the attention that will help you later in dealing with the media and the public.[75]

Incidentally, Tea Campaign's first attempt at setting its own stage outside the university was a total failure. We picked out Berlin's Winterfeld Market, known for its charm and located in a section of the city where we thought customers would be open to the idea of our Tea Campaign. To get a stand, you had to turn up shortly before 6:00 AM on Saturday morning and be inspected by the official Cerberus who had the power over the market. He assigned us a space for a stand, and we stepped up with our homemade signs and a table covered with wallpaper. The market master didn't like "students," that is, anyone who looked skinny, intellectual and "unconventional." And he liked us even less when we dared to argue with him. At this time he was also no longer sober, which made dealing with him a tad difficult. In brief, he amused himself mightily by assigning us a space between the two portable toilets, where we then stood with our "Darjeeling First Flush Finest Tippy Golden Flowery Orange Pekoe." The world's best tea in this environment! It took us much too long to eliminate the Winterfeld Market from our repertoire. Many of the people in Berlin who know us from those first days think that we're a small alternative or student project, and ask with concern whether we're still around.

8.4.4 ... but you can also do without

Sometimes you don't need any marketing at all – when you stay within your own group. Within your own circle of friends. In your own part of town or your own household. In your club or association. Then you'll save yourself a big chunk of expenses, which for a good many products makes up the biggest part of the price. Cosmetics are a well-known example of this; basically they're products for which a "brand" has been built with a lot of money. But you, too, can establish something quite exclusive, but something quite different. As in the following story.

It begins with the founding of Schloss [Castle, Château] Vaux in Berlin in 1868. In the years that followed, a company purchased the Château de Vaux and the adjoining vineyards located not far from Metz on the Moselle, establishing a German champagne house. For 50 years the Château was the basis for production, but then the owners had to give up their French residence. The company's new headquarters are in the "city of roses," Eltville on the Rhine. From then on Schloss Vaux has specialized in the Rheingau and making sparkling wines out of its best grapes.

In 1982 a small and exclusive circle of friends came together and purchased Schloss Vaux from a subsidiary of the Deutsche Bank. Gustav Adolf Schaeling, a bank president from Wiesbaden, chaired the board of directors and began to breathe new life into the famed champagne maker. Four years later, the partners converted the champagne producer into a stock corporation. A group of 60 shareholders was formed, all aficionados of Rheingau sparkling wines. Since then the group has been meeting once a year in elegant private surroundings – and as a dividend, the shareholders take home bottles of the noble libation. How did I get to know the story? The general manager of a well-known business association requested entry into this exclusive group and received a polite rejection: additional shareholders, he was told, are not desired, nor is an expansion of the business model.

If you stay within your own group, you don't need marketing.

8.5 The Idea of Building with Bottles

What comes to mind when you see a bottle? You'll find the design of the bottle attractive or not; perhaps the color appeals to you, or perhaps you consider whether it might work as a decorative element. I have often thought about these designs and asked myself why no one has developed a much more obvious form, that is, a form that would permit bottles to be used as building blocks. One might consider glass, but also PET or earthenware as materials.

Glass blocks would be particularly suitable for Central Europe since our region is short on light and warmth. Clear glass bottles offer both. Put together to form walls, they would create rooms with lots of light, and double or triple glass windows would insulate well. Instead of melting the glass to recycle it, you would give the bottles a *second economic life*, and an extraordinary one at that. The whole thing would be free – an ideal building material. Squared into blocks, with the neck of one bottle inserted into the base of the next bottle, the glass bottles would fit together securely. I'm not thinking of those unimaginative glass brick walls from the 1960s, but of very clear, high quality bottles that would make it possible to construct an aesthetically pleasant building.

To prevent overheating the rooms, you could cover the walls with plants on the outside. People planning to build themselves a house would drink out of rationally designed bottles for as long as it took to collect the building material. That material wouldn't be financed by a bank but would come from your own storage space, or if you yourself were not planning to build, some publicly accessible space where people could put their bottles so that other people who wanted to build could get them as free building material. I see whole villages arising before my eyes, created out of imaginatively shaped igloos or houses with vertical glass walls and wooden roof beams, all taking advantage of light and warmth. I've never understood why designers are hired to come up with the most eccentric forms, who yet leave the simplest and best forms unrealized.

I know the German building code won't allow these bottle structures. The situation is similar in neighboring countries. In the tropics, on the other hand, it would get too hot in a glass or PET house. I know there have been efforts to build houses out of existing glass bottles, but I've found nothing in the literature where radically redesigned bottles have been conceived of as building blocks. Apparently there are conventions as to what a beverage bottle should look like, and these conventions don't favor the simple shape that could be used as a building block. Personally, I'd find it extremely stylish to have square bottles gracing my table. Well, at least one part of the idea has been realized with mustard jars, through subsequent use as drinking glasses. With bottle houses, homeless or slum shacks made of cardboard, leftover wood and corrugated sheet metal would soon disappear. Instead, there would be much more useful and more elegant glass houses.

Yes, you surmise correctly, I've been thinking about this idea for a while. I've even filed a patent application. Title: "Containers for Liquids," application date, May 20, 1996.[76] But there hasn't been anything beyond the application because the costs for the next steps seemed too high, and I couldn't imagine that a patent would be given for such a simple idea. At home I have piles of cardboard models for building blocks from bottles and models for roof tiles where the opening of the bottle is in the shape of a boss for securing it to the roof battens. It's a real collection of containers which I've gathered over the course of years and which come close to the idea of glass building blocks. I have occupied myself intensively with this idea, but a truly coherent concept still eludes me. Not all ideas result in a usable outcome; others just take a long time giving birth.

9 Entrepreneurship as a Challenge

Never have the conditions for successfully implementing one's own ideas been as favorable as they are today. Modern markets, contracted services and the Internet make it possible for small companies and one-man/one-woman businesses to become viable market players with calculable financial outlays.

"Why wait to get laid off?" was the title of an article in *Brigitte*, a German women's magazine. This article recommends that in these times of outsourcing and lean management, its readers should unshackle themselves from their employers and earn their income using what they've gotten from their companies – knowledge and experience.

The first intelligent step in the direction of entrepreneurship is *not* to identify where we could earn money, but rather to discover what ideas and visions of our own we can generate. Entrepreneurship has the potential to be much more than self-employment: a passion, a journey of self-discovery, even a calling; a challenge to commit yourself to your own dreams, to achieve self-realization in your work and to accomplish something great. Achieving economic success will follow, because what we do out of inner conviction and with all our strength will be work of the highest quality we are capable of. Recent neurobiological research even suggests that what we do with passion enhances the quality of certain brain functions.[77]

To begin with, there has to be an idea. "What's missing where? What do I want to improve? What am I shooting for?"

But if money is the only motivation ("how can I make a lot of money as quickly as possible?"), we shouldn't be surprised if we rarely come up with something original or really useful. The question is much too limited. You won't succeed this way. This might even explain another phenomenon: when we're presented with so many attractive goods, objects of desire for those who don't have them, we nonetheless can't rid ourselves of the feeling that many of these objects and the lifestyles they help to generate are actually missing our needs by a hair.

Let there be no misunderstanding: this is not intended as moralizing. Absolutely not; attitudes of moral superiority are deeply suspect to me. A business founder should earn money – and plenty of it. He should be remunerated for the risks and lean times he's willing to take on. It's my fervent wish that as many founders as possible are financially successful. Entrepreneurship creates prosperity. The pie gets bigger, and whoever helps make it bigger has earned the right to a big slice of it for himself or herself.

My criticism isn't directed against profit; it's directed against the meaningless fixation on profit to the exclusion of all else. Where market principles are betrayed, profit loses its guiding function, its function as the benchmark for the satisfaction of needs and achievement of efficiency. I am invoking the tradition in economic thought that doesn't regard economics as an activity that in itself conveys meaning, but as an activity to serve mankind. Meaning doesn't arise from economic principles. Profit enables the pursuit of meaning, not the other way around. The economy is the means of eliminating heavy physical labor, economic hardship, and disease. Profit is the *engine* for economic development, but it doesn't belong in the driver's seat. Economics is not competent when it comes to the essential questions of human development. This has remained the consensus in the discipline of economics to this day. The justified criticisms of many of its manifestations in practice should not mislead us to damn economics across the board. Consensus has become a valuable commodity. At this point we should not be giving it up.

9.1 Stand Up for Something – Support a Cause

> If you want to live a happy life,
> tie it to a goal ...
>
> ALBERT EINSTEIN

Numbers are seldom the object of passion. It is more likely that people yearn to commit themselves to a meaningful task. You only have to give them the opportunity. Do something meaningful; it 's a persuasive formula for success to stand for something. Guy Kawasaki[78], a veteran start-up entrepreneur and consultant who played an important role in Apple's early history, made the same point, adding, "It took me 20 years to come to this conclusion ."

Textbooks take it for granted that a founder's main motivation is profit. However, case studies of successful start-ups as well as the biographies of numerous entrepreneurs tell us something different. For example, Karl Vesper, an American professor who has analyzed more than 100 start-ups, observes, "Most entrepreneurs who are successful have concepts that are not only sound business models, but are also in harmony with their personal attitudes, desired lifestyle and values."[79]

Above all, you want to create something you are proud of.... That has always been my philosophy of business. I can honestly say that I have never gone into any business purely to make money. If that is the sole motive, then I believe you are better off doing nothing, commented Virgin founder Richard Branson. A business has to be involving; it has to be fun, and it has to exercise your creative instincts.[80]

9.2 The Myth of Profit Maximization

Branson's point of view coincides with that of Richard Ohlson, the founder of the Swiss Research Institute for Applied Economics, who noted, "Anyone who is only after the money doesn't have the stamina you need to be a successful entrepreneur." More detailed studies on the principle of profit maximization as the motivating factor confirm these observations. Jacobsen summarizes empirical findings in her dissertation as follows: "Surprisingly, and this is important, precisely this type of economic success seems to have been the decisive factor for very few people to start up businesses. Much more frequently, what is important to them is a non-economic dimension that goes beyond the immediate improvement of their economic situation; that is, if they succeed in developing their abilities and putting their ideas into action, they 'become their own boss,' achieving in this way spiritual and physical comfort in the form of self-fulfillment."[81] According to Jacobsen, the inner sense of having accomplished something best explains why entrepreneurs are often not striving for money or income as such, but instead consider financial success merely as a measure and confirmation of their own performance.[82]

The futurist Matthias Horx recognizes a trend here that will become increasingly important. According to Horx, our individualistic culture will produce a type of entrepreneur who will be connected to his work on a dimension that goes beyond money, that is, a business owner who wants to become good because he is ambitious – but ambitious in a new sense; he wants to shape his life as a work of art that is as coherent and interesting as possible.[83]

The exclusive orientation to sales and profit is increasingly proving to be a deterrent to entrepreneurial success. At the beginning of the 21st century, successful companies prevail not solely through business acumen, but also through forward-looking ideas, willingness to assume responsibility, and sensitivity to social values. Their leaders aren't mere idealists, but are actually very successful founders who don't have money as their primary incentive. In other words, a shot of idealism is apparently a splendid prerequisite for a successful start-up.

This has immediate socio-political significance. Many potential founders are frightened off by the erroneous assumption that profit must be the sole motivating force – as if that were an absolute necessity. Actually, the opposite is true. There is solid evidence for the hypothesis that a good idea or commitment to a good cause enhances prospects for success rather than diminishing them.

Examples of this abound in other areas. People who choose the fields of artistic endeavor or sports or commitment to social issues do not – at least primarily – choose these fields for the money that success might bring them. Not because this would be morally reprehensible, but because it wouldn't fulfill their essential needs. Artistic creativity, athletic performance and social challenges are fascinating because they promise a life with a bit of an edge, because you can achieve self-actualization in all the fibers of your being, or because you can at least be part of the scene. Entrepreneurial initiatives are in demand in areas where they have previously not been applied. What is needed is the *citoyen,* the engaged citizen, as entrepreneur and artist, someone who can win back those social, emotional and intellectual qualities that have been lost. What the world wants are people who make meaningful work possible both for themselves and for others: in short, the imaginative transformation of our livelihood through a more open and rich culture of entrepreneurship.

9.3 Social Entrepreneurship

The idea of social entrepreneurship is gaining ground around the world. This is probably because the concept of commitment to a social cause is linked to the idea of entrepreneurial initiatives, purposeful organization and disciplined cost management on the part of companies. Something along the lines of Richard Branson and Mother Teresa in one and the same person. Moreover, the concept responds to a movement that acknowledges that governments, administrations and existing social organizations do not seem to be coming to grips with certain types of problems, whether because they function inefficiently, are administering rather than satisfying social needs, or because they are simply rigid and obsolete. We need, so goes the thesis, "social entrepreneurs," who with new approaches to complex new problems will find and implement suitable answers.

The term "social entrepreneurship" is new, but the concept is not. There have always been social entrepreneurs, and many of our institutions originated because of them. Back in the 19th century, Friedrich von Bodelschwingh created the Bethel Institute in Germany, a world-renowned social enterprise that functioned according to economic principles and operated its own artisan workshops, its own electric and water supply, its own schools and training centers.

The founder of the Red Cross, Henri Dunant, was most certainly a social entrepreneur, as was Mother Teresa in Calcutta.

A contemporary and fascinating example of a social entrepreneur is Andreas Heinecke. His work with the blind arose from his observation that the real barrier in interacting with disabled persons lies in people's heads. It is prejudice and fear that block connecting and exchanging ideas with the handicapped. Heinecke's answer to this was the exhibit "Dialogue in the Dark" – a model that plunges sighted people into darkness, to be led by the blind and learn new ways of seeing. "Dialogue in the Dark" represents a unique system of integration whose goal is to overcome prejudices while at the same time avoiding pity as much as possible. The handicapped stand in the foreground with their abilities rather than with their disabilities. The project's success lies in returning disadvantaged groups to a place in society.

Beyond their already impressive social commitment, social entrepreneurs create concepts that didn't exist previously and put them into practice successfully.

It is also true that social entrepreneurs are pioneers who work with new approaches instead of attempting to improve existing processes through minor changes. So it's not a matter of what the English-speaking world calls "best practice," but rather of creating new concepts to solve social problems.

Muhammad Yunus is a good example. His Grameen Bank with its microcredit revolutionized the understanding and practice of granting loans. *Prior to* Yunus, the poor were not deemed creditworthy but, perhaps even more importantly, they weren't profitable customers for the banks even if they did repay their loans, because in the conventional banking system very small loans created a disproportionately high administrative burden. And of course no one believed that the poor possessed the skills needed by entrepreneurs. Yunus created a totally new approach, proving that the poor are a good credit risk and that it's possible to create a system that is mostly self-financing, that charges and collects interest and is applicable internationally. Anyone familiar with the Yunus story knows that he began with a loan of about $27, a ridiculously small sum by our standards, to help 42 women achieve micro-entrepreneurship (*i.e.*, a little bit more than 50 cents per project), and that without exception all the borrowers repaid their loans.

I invite you to join me in thinking how we might better understand this new discipline of social entrepreneurship and how to better publicize its opportunities and conditions.

Normally, when we discuss entrepreneurship, we ask: how do *new* things come into the world? We discuss future developments, innovations and marketing strategies.

Now let's ask ourselves: how do *good* things come into the world? Perhaps you'll say there are people with good intentions and others with bad intentions. In the case of entrepreneurship, that would mean that the "good guys" pursue social entrepreneurship and the "bad guys" do business entrepreneurship. The good guys altruistically commit themselves to other people for good objectives, while the bad guys commit themselves to the worship of Mammon.

Much that you hear in popular discussions about business runs along these lines. It's as if profit were the mark of Cain by which you can distinguish the good guys from the bad. Of course this is more than simplistic. Today, even hardcore non-profit folks recognize that it's good to earn surpluses and employ them for your purposes.

> "Twenty years ago the idea of nonprofits acting in an entrepreneurial manner was anathema to most people in the sector: The idea of merging mission and money filled them with distaste."
>
> BOSCHEE/McCLURG

Profits: yes or no? I am afraid this question won't get us any further. We have to delve more deeply into the motivations of the actors. Let me share a little story to illuminate this issue.

Harvard, July 1998. Howard Stevenson, professor of entrepreneurship, is reporting on a new teaching module for this venerable institution. Ethical conduct, he says, is now a component of management education. You can't start teaching these principles to your economics students soon enough. He stresses emphatically how important the ethical conduct of its students is to an educational institution – especially after the numerous corporate scandals in the US. Then Stevenson stops speaking. There's a long pause. A few of his listeners grow uneasy, especially as the professor stands before them red-faced and looking somewhat unwell. He simply stands there, silently. Perhaps a minute passes, an eternity. As his audience starts to become concerned, he calmly continues, "Is there anyone here in this room foolish enough to believe you could do it like this?" Create ethical conduct through instruction?

Haven't there been many others preaching ethics before? Professor Stevenson was right – it isn't that simple. Stevenson proposed that we examine the situation more closely, analyze the motives and try to figure out how we can create a win-win situation.

Permit me to formulate several heretical theses that address the motivations of good people and bad, but especially the good. There's a substantial literature describing how "good" people don't act solely on altruistic principle, but also pursue goals out of self-interest, whether simply for self-satisfaction, seeking recognition in the community, the desire for meaningful work, the need to achieve something positive, or perhaps even out of the desire to attain a lofty position, be it by way of public recognition or in a leadership position in a charitable organization. Not to mention that it can also be a matter of preserving one's own job. There's absolutely nothing limiting or even negative about this. I only mean that such a motivational assessment is more realistic and more accurate than focusing solely on the altruistic aspects. (You're invited to dispute this vigorously!)

But, please, don't misunderstand me. I don't want to say anything ironic or disparaging about the so-called "good people" as often happens in public debate. That's not my intent. I'm only advocating for a closer look at motivation. And also for the possibility of finding "good people" in places where we generally don't expect to find them.

Now let's take a look at the "bad guys." As we saw in the first section, business entrepreneurship is often distinguished from social entrepreneurship through its profit motive.

But, as we know, profits don't fall from heaven. You have to work for them and, while doing so, you encounter very special conditions. And I believe one can state as a general rule that today there is a whole array of trends at work that make it more and more difficult to persist in unscrupulous business practices over the long term.

Why ethical conduct is beginning to pay off

- ✔ Level of education is rising
- ✔ Competition is increasing; markets are becoming more transparent
- ✔ Opportunities for comparison are improving (comparison testing, the Internet)
- ✔ "Ethics pays" is becoming more realistic, since unscrupulous business dealings may be getting more difficult.

So, even if we're to assume that the wicked are up to no good, market conditions have a tendency to enforce "good" conduct. This, in fact, is the thesis of Adam Smith's famous book *The Wealth of Nations* (1776): participation in the market has the potential to improve one's moral character. Understood in this way, as part of a long tradition of economic thought, doing good can be said to appeal to our "enlightened self-interest," rather than pure altruism.

"Ethics pays" has become a component of management literature.

A company's good will, confidence in its products and positive references in the media, are increasingly valuable, indeed almost priceless. The Brent Spar affair, when Shell was trying to dump a decommissioned oil platform into the North Sea, was the turning point in matters of corporate policy and consumer power. It demonstrated that even large corporations like Shell are forced to bend under the pressure of public opinion. So much for the more objective side of the "evil business entrepreneur."

But what about its subjective side?

The popular interpretation of the discipline of economics trots out *homo oeconomicus*, a kind of Frankenstein monster without feelings and soul, obsessed solely by profit. But this fails to recognize that in its practice economics, like every other academic discipline, abstracts its subject matter from an abundance of circumstantial factors. *Homo oeconomicus* is only a model, a premise, not a description of reality. Economics students learn this in their first semester. Humans are made of flesh and blood, and of course they have more than purely economic goals. The same holds true for entrepreneurs. We explained in the preceding chapters that successful businesses require individuals who are more than mere profit maximizers. Naturally, a desire for recognition, for something spectacular, for independence and success, also plays a role. Money and accumulated wealth are only markers of success. The generation of the founders frequently lives a frugal lifestyle.

What I want to say is this: the difference between social entrepreneurs and business entrepreneurs is much smaller than people think. In fact, we may be witnessing a convergence: budget cuts for social services will force social entrepreneurs to resort more and more to methods of efficiency and market orientation, while increasing information, transparency, competition and opportunities for comparison will force business entrepreneurs to offer good products and honest services, if they wish to be economically successful over the long term.

According to business consultant Gareth Morgan, "Being in harmony with social values is a prerequisite for success." As Morgan puts it, "Entrepreneurial ideas must be interwoven with social values and problems," and "Indifference to social problems frightens people, undermines their confidence and almost always backfires with a negative effect, at least in the long run."[84] These days, entrepreneurs must provide a much greater degree of responsibility, but this doesn't require equally high moral motivations – only the desire for survival and success. Thus you could say that business entrepreneurs are, *in their own best interests,* moving in the direction of the social entrepreneurs. Well-functioning markets are creating mechanisms that tend to compel good conduct. Good conduct is an essential feature of functioning societies.

I'd like to bring up a third point relating to the prospects for social entrepreneurship. The expansion of the concept of entrepreneurship into the social arena could have the result that people skeptical of business become more open to entrepreneurship as an activity that is more creative and congenial than the business of large, anonymous companies and multinationals.

> Social entrepreneurship is as important for the development of societies as entrepreneurship is for the development of the economy.
>
> ROGER MARTIN/SALLY OSBURG
> "Social Entrepreneurship: The Case for Definition,"
> *Stanford Social Innovation Review* 2007

9.4 Must You be Born an Entrepreneur?

Do you have to be born an entrepreneur? It's a widespread view that an entrepreneur must possess a whole array of personality traits if he wants to be successful. Assertiveness, self-sufficiency (high internal locus of control), business skills and expertise, tenacity, rhetorical ability, and more. This all sounds very reasonable. Nonetheless, it's not true.

There have been numerous empirical studies, particularly in the USA, which ask what personality traits make a successful entrepreneur. It turned out in these studies that there's *no* empirical evidence for these apparently reasonable character traits. Surprisingly, the "traits approach" shows no specific traits for successful start-up entrepreneurs.[85] In spite of intensive research it hasn't yet been possible to identify either a single personality trait or a composite of character traits by which you could predict either start-up activities or their success.[86]

There are no predetermined character traits for start-up entrepreneurs that would permit a prediction of their business success. The notion that qualities like assertiveness and leadership skills evolve over time is not unreasonable, but it would be wrong to regard these traits as the basis for success and assume that they are indispensible from the start.[87]

It follows that many more individuals are qualified to become business founders than is generally thought, and we can cast the net much wider when it comes to thinking about a broader, more open entrepreneurial culture. Entrepreneurship is not a specialized field accessible to only the few and with entrée only through a set of special skills. No exceptional traits are required up front for you to succeed as a founder.[88] Another conventional belief that prevents us from giving birth to many more innovative start-ups is one we have already encountered: the belief that you need a brilliant inspiration. Other than a few lucky devils, not many people have such brilliant inspirations. "I'm just an ordinary person. What about me?"

9.4.1 "Much Too Difficult?"

Rangsdorf School, October 2004. "Much too difficult for middle schoolers ," was the teachers' initial assessment when Sven Ripsas and I were preparing the first workshop for the German branch of the National Foundation for Teaching Entrepreneurship (NFTE). "You're going to crash and burn with your workshop." The teachers from the middle schools involved in the project could not imagine that their students would take to the subject matter. "Middle school students aren't interested in starting businesses."

That last sentence made us sit up and take notice. "Could be that the students won't listen if we only tell them about our own experiences," we thought, "but starting a company, what's boring about that?"

It turned out very differently. Of course we didn't drone on endlessly with long lectures. Instead we gave them a few examples and questions, questions, questions. "What do you do in your spare time?" "What do you spend your money on?" "What do you get for it?" "Is it good or not so good?" "Could you do it better?" "What would you need if you wanted to do it better?" Or also: "What do you especially like to do?" "Could you earn money doing it?" "What would that have to look like?" "What would you need to do it?" "Where would you get the expertise?" "Who would have to help you to do it?" "How could you arrange for this help?" During the break, one of the students remarked that at school no one ever asked them anything; they just had to learn things. He had been afraid that at the workshop they were going to have to "learn" things again.

The students were supposed to think up something for themselves. Either something they'd like to do, or maybe something they could already do a little bit, something that would make sense to the other students, parents and friends, in the neighborhood. This was their first tentative attempt to come up with an "entrepreneurial idea." Many of the students found this very difficult. They'd start with an idea and then discover they had run up against difficulties. And then they'd give up. We asked probing questions and had them explain the difficulties to us. Often just by describing the difficulty they got an idea how they might overcome it. Or they'd ask us what we thought of an idea. As if they had to get our permission and we were the authority that knew whether the idea would work or not. We explained there wasn't anyone who really knew that; they'd have to judge for themselves whether a little idea like that was worth something or not. That was totally new. It appeared that their opinion wasn't otherwise much in demand. Sophie remarked thoughtfully, "I always thought anybody who thought up a great business idea had to be a very special person. But your examples showed us you don't have to be a genius. You just have to let your imagination run free, work on your idea and not let yourself be easily discouraged by anyone."

Gradually little entrepreneurial concepts started peeling out of the group. A number of the students rode motor scooters and had financial problems when their scooters were in the repair shop. Couldn't you fix them yourself? Not really, but there were friends and acquaintances who could help you. The idea of a scooter repair shop was taking form. A number of the students had already purchased replacement parts and tried to put them in themselves. Now they could buy these parts together, maybe at a wholesaler, and save money. Another member of the group chimed in, "Every time I want to drink a cola it's awfully expensive. But we could drink our own colas at the repair shop, and when friends stop by, we could sell them cola much cheaper than at the stand." A scooter repair shop –with beverage service.

Clothing also fired up the imagination. T-shirts, for example. Cut holes in them, whipstitch the sleeves or print them with wild graffiti.

The ideas were presented on the afternoon of the third day. NFTE insisted that the students make their presentations with PowerPoints. Totally new for the students and not an easy job. Even we were skeptical whether they would succeed in this Herculean effort. Then it was time. The jury included prestigious names, such as Stephen Brenninkmeijer from the C&A dynasty and chairman of the Board of NFTE Germany. The work continued hectically up until the last moment; many of the ideas were quickly reworked or reformulated. One student began to cry because she didn't think her idea was convincing any more.

The presentation began. All the students were present, and 19 concepts were presented. Each one was feasible, manageable and taken from the student's own life experience. One of the students had come up with particularly bizarre graffiti for his T-shirt production. In support of his idea he commented, "There's nothing half way decent in the stores.

When I go to C&A – everything is so boring!" The student didn't have a clue who was sitting in front of him. The teachers laugh, and we do too. So does Stephen Brenninkmeijer. He likes the designs.

Naturally we know a workshop like this is a special situation, well prepared and well equipped, and with unusual concern for the participants, conditions that middle schools will not easily be able to replicate under current circumstances. Even though we want to be cautious about drawing conclusions from a single stand-alone workshop, I think founding a company is a good topic, even for middle schoolers. Not only because one initiative or another might grow out of it but, more importantly, as an unconventional learning experience for the students that builds their self-confidence and encourages them to undertake more than they would have done otherwise.

9.4.2 What Matters: Not the Resources but the Concept

Attempts to determine through *tests* who is suited to be a business founder have also been fruitless. The evidence suggests that the skills we ascribe to founders arise only through the process, that is, in the course of running the business.[89]

I can confirm this from my own observations. More than once I've seen that people without apparent promise have turned out to be exceptional at starting up their own companies. Convinced that they have a well thought-out and dynamic concept, they put it into practice with great will and tenacity. Take, for example, my student Kurt. He was obsessed with the idea that he could make rock concerts cheaper so that young people without much money could attend them. His idea was to have performances by groups that didn't yet have big names, but which he believed were promising new directions in rock.

Kurt himself was a lone wolf, who found scarcely any support among his fellow students for himself or for his idea.

So he bugged me to get him the university's big auditorium for a Rock Night. I didn't find Kurt particularly congenial either. I had only a rudimentary idea of what he wanted to do because he couldn't express it clearly. Only his stubbornness and insistence made it clear that he had worked on the idea and was committed to it. To make a long story short, I was able to persuade the university administration to permit the experiment. The very first Rock Night was well attended, and my own apprehensions and prejudices against such events proved to be unfounded.

A second Rock Night followed close on the heels of the first and sold out. The third Rock Night was so popular that we narrowly sidestepped a disaster. The attendees stormed up onto a stage that was approved for only a small number of people and threatened to collapse. In my desperation – I was fully liable for everything – I grabbed a fire-breather who had been hired as intermission entertainment and, with his help, was able to shoo people off the stage.

Kurt's concept was a big hit. The entrance fee of five Deutschmarks back at that time was more than enough to cover the cost of the event, including the money for the bands. The musicians were good and became better known through this first gig. One of Kurt's singers was Herbert Grönemeyer, virtually unknown at the time, and now a household name in Germany.

Kurt's success still didn't get him the respect of his fellow students. On the contrary, a group of students demanded that they, too, be given the chance to hold an event like this. According to them, a concert like that was really easy, and whatever Kurt could do, they could do as well. So another event was held under the same conditions, an event that even enjoyed the added advantage of being a benefit concert in support of the Sandinistas in Nicaragua (then popular among left-leaning students in Berlin). But despite great effort, considerable money spent, and the flavor of political correctness, the concert barely recouped its expenses. Typical: the resources (i.e. the concert venue) were thought to be most important, not the concept. "If only we had had the big auditorium, we could have done it, too." Well, they did have the big auditorium. But it was Kurt's idea, his intuition for good but not yet well-known musicians, in short, his concept, that made the difference.

9.5 The World Needs Entrepreneurs

In German society, but really everywhere, there are many creative people who have good ideas they'd like to implement, and who perhaps are already doing so with great commitment in political parties, associations, clubs or as volunteers. But they scarcely ever think that they could also pursue such activities in the form of entrepreneurship, with financial goals for themselves.

The conventional notion about founders has long imagined people who put on a tie, foster good relations with banks, fill out long application forms, even take out a mortgage on Grandma's house, and then, equipped with business administration expertise and bank loan or other support, take the step of starting their own business.

And just as business plan competitions focus on business administration topics, this practice is reinforced in many start-up seminars and publications. Result: the small trickle of potential business founders becomes even thinner. Most business consultants don't even mention factors like creativity, passion or commitment as prerequisites for start-up entrepreneurs. It's as if they simply had no role to play. Even though many successful business owners emphasize these facets of their own personality either explicitly or implicitly, these attributes are accorded little importance in the conventional research. Instead of the sheer lust for profit that is taken for granted, for many entrepreneurs it is the desire for adventure or love of a challenge that gets them going. Richard Branson, the colorful founder of Virgin Records, writes in his autobiography:

"I am often asked why I go in for record-breaking challenges with either powerboats or hot-air balloons. People point out that, with success, money and a happy family, I should stop putting myself and them at risk and enjoy what I am so lucky to have. This is obvious truth, and part of me wholeheartedly agrees with it. I love life; I love my family and I am horrified by the idea of being killed and leaving Joan without a husband and Holly and Sam without a father. But another part of me is driven to try new adventures and I still find that I want to push myself to my limits."[90]

There is much to suggest that entrepreneurs can live a freer, more intense and probably more fulfilled life than many of their contemporaries. To be sure, few people possess such extreme personalities as Richard Branson; nevertheless, many of the better-known founders are free spirits, with a personality profile closer to artists than to managers and bookkeepers.

> Skill is not the answer, neither is money.
>
> What you need is optimism, humanism, enthusiasm, intuition, curiosity, love, humor, magic and fun and that secret ingredient-euphoria.
>
> None of this appears on the curriculum of any business school.
>
> ANNITA RODDICK

9.6 Entrepreneurship as an Adventure

The thrill that many people seek in an adventure vacation can also be found through entrepreneurship, through innovative and – at times – extravagant professional work. The strains of wage labor are inadequately mitigated by the worker's focus on vacation. What makes a vacation exciting for a short time could instead be used to make work more fulfilling throughout the entire year.

The core of entrepreneurship is creativity. I know many entrepreneurs who simply don't know what to do with themselves on a conventional vacation of the type regular employees typically and ardently yearn for. Anyone who is not consumed by business administration can spend time at the beach, vacation or not, if that helps him sort out his ideas and mentally transform them into new entrepreneurial designs. He won't consider this as *lost* time, however, but as an *investment* in the concept of his company. I feel sorry for people who need vacations – by now, my entire life is a vacation, more intense and more varied than in the past. Creating a new business model of my own is more thrilling for me than reading a detective story or going to the movies. You give birth to your entrepreneurial babies and follow their development. It's incredibly enriching, lively and exciting – just as it is with your real children.

My personal method of working creatively is to walk through nature. If the beach and palm trees attracted me, I'd go for walks there. I've never been able to hold out for more than five minutes on a beach chair or in a hammock. Presumably everyone has to find his own ideal creative environment. The Danish philosopher Kierkegaard needed his six stand-up desks. They say that while World Chess Master Bobby Fischer was pondering his next move, he had himself driven around the city in a taxi. A famous Buddhist monk is said to have had his crucial inspirations while he was tinkling.

There are better options than working for someone else. The jobs that were once disparaged as wage labor now run the risk of being glorified. Suddenly wage labor is becoming something valuable.

I remember well: until the 1960s the highest wages in Germany were paid to miners. The argument used by the miners' union, IG Bergbau, to justify and legitimize these wages was that work in the mines was hell on earth. Heat, dust, hard physical labor and workplace risks were manifestations of this hell. And work in this hell had to be compensated materially. That made sense to me. Since that time the mining lobby has worked hand in hand with the union to maintain coal mining. For half a century the mining industry, *i.e.*, the embodiment of hell, has been heavily subsidized by the taxpayer. Have we all gone crazy? Or has the argument for saving jobs simply blinded us?

This is why the work by Frithjof Bergmann[91] deserves more respect. Today, he says, you have the opportunity to say goodbye to the "silent disease of wage labor" and to create a job for yourself that's more satisfying than what most companies are offering to its employees. In *New Work, New Culture* Bergmann explains that today the technical prerequisites exist for organizing production in a decentralized fashion, that is, in small, self-determined units.

Take charge of your own life, and don't let it be controlled by others.

Interestingly, you can pursue entrepreneurship even without founding a company of your own. Instead of responding to job announcements and getting into a long line of job seekers, you can also use good entrepreneurial design to position yourself outside the box of a job description. Then what is foregrounded is not the educational system's certificate, but a well-developed concept, offered to an existing organization as an opportunity for innovation. A personnel director will think twice before he turns down an "applicant" who comes with an original concept in hand and a promise to implement it. After all, it could turn out that this concept makes a big splash at the competition.

This would be a direct transfer of education into economic innovation, with no detour through instructional subjects, certificates and job titles. Not a bad alternative at a time when fulfilling jobs, well-remunerated and secure, are becoming rarer and rarer. A kind of *Intrapreneurship*,[92] if you wish to describe it that way.[93] "If you hire me, I'm willing to contribute my concept for the benefit of your company." A very attractive offer for the company, especially if it happens to be producing very few innovations in-house. Any job applicant who takes this approach is signaling that s/he has learned to think entrepreneurially. This can work for entrepreneurs who don't want to bother with the formalities of setting up a company of their own. Entrepreneurship approached in this manner definitely sidesteps business administration, since those tasks will be assumed by the existing company.

In contrast to these approaches, the *dream of owning your own business* often carries notions that don't mesh with reality. "Being your own boss" is not always the path to bliss. Many people discover that they end up working harder and are burdened with more responsibility than their own employees. In addition, there's the uncertainty of success, given the empirically established high failure rate. By itself, the idea of being the boss isn't worth much if it's not based on a mature concept that responds to actual market conditions and fits with the character of the founder.

Why else would successful founders write books like *Business is like Rock and Roll* (Richard Branson), *The Lazy Way to Succeed* (Fred Gratzon) or *Success at Life: How to Catch and Live your Dream* (Ron Rubin), just to name three? Founding a company doesn't necessarily mean a 16-hour day filled with business administration tasks. It's time we killed this ghost.

9.7 The Individual Takes Center Stage

When I think about students of mine who have founded a company or who are on their way to doing so, I find something else worth noting. It's not just that new companies with better products and services have come into being. New people have also emerged from the process: "new" in the sense that their personalities have developed positively. They're more focused, better learners and better communicators. They're more optimistic and better able to meet life's challenges. They're even better looking! Naturally, you'll say, success is good for people. But there is more to it than that.

If you ask me today what works best for personality development, I'll simply say that it's entrepreneurship. Nothing even remotely comparable has had a more positive effect on the personalities of my students. The process starts with the individual beginning to focus. Even in my own case, with my tea idea, I suddenly developed a "tea focus." Without any effort, I absorbed everything that had to do with tea. In a row of stores my eyes would gravitate to the tea shops. I studied the displays like a child and absorbed many details, building up knowledge and expertise . No "tea course," *no learning sequence no matter how vivid,* could have been more effective. Suddenly my attention gained direction and purpose.

I observed the same phenomenon in my students, who began to develop a goal-oriented vision, a sustained interest in a subject. This focusing didn't seem to compete much with their academic activities, but rather with their goofing-off time. Where other young people or adults pass their time in inconsequential activity, those who have gotten a little taste of entrepreneurship create idea concepts and design their own economic future. All because they themselves want to do this. Modern pedagogy calls this "self-directed learning."

If you look at entrepreneurship in this way, you see that the figure of the founder has moved closer to the center. In an older view, the founder was the figure who implements business administration thinking – less important as a unique personality, possibly even a distraction. Best, really, to replace this figure with mathematical formulas and a computer; discipline then would never be a problem, and personal inclinations and emotions would not interfere with optimally organized processes. Of course this is a bit of a caricature – but over time considerations like these made it possible for business administration studies to diminish the importance of the figure of the founder. Putting that figure back in the center encourages us to see the work of the entrepreneur in the same light in which the university reformer Humboldt saw the work of the academy.

> The destination of humanity
> is the education of the individual
> into a harmonious work of art,
> a personality developed in all its talents, with
> a positive perspective on all aspects of the world
>
> WILHELM V. HUMBOLDT

If the focus is on ideas, especially ideas that are original or represent new, creative combinations, then the individual becomes key to the game again. "The essence of entrepreneurship is being different," says Marc Casson.[94] Being different than the others makes the difference.

The Austrian economist Joseph Schumpeter (1883-1950), who taught at Oxford, Cambridge and Harvard universities, was the first to have presented the figure of the businessman as a key element of economic life.[95] Of course there were entrepreneurs earlier on, but economists considered it progressive to be independent of the always already unpredictable individual. Science: an endeavor to develop general premises that abstract from the individuality of the persons involved. Where profit maximization is the single goal, the thinking went, either as the underlying motive, or because the market requires it, you can get by with optimizing business functions, independent of the person who carries them out. Why bother to worry about the individual?

That's why Schumpeter is being rediscovered: because it turns out that entrepreneurs are made of flesh and blood and not all from the same mold; that many cutting-edge ideas do not arise in big organizations , but in the heads of mavericks and non-conformists. Fresh beginnings, unusual and untested ideas, risks with the threat of failure – all of this demands something different than a focus on business functions.

Schumpeter divided business leaders into two camps, the managers and the innovative entrepreneurs. In the first camp he put the established companies protecting their markets, while he saw the driving force for an economy coming from the second camp, the aggressors who were forcing their way into the market with new products or processes. The better is the enemy of the existing. Consequently Schumpeter spoke of "creative destruction."

While banquet speakers cannot say enough good things about innovation , they're strangely silent regarding "creative destruction." Schumpeter is cited by politicians of all stripes, but the consequences of his ideas are swept under the carpet.

9.8 Why We Create: It's About Efficiency

A McKinsey consultant knocks on heaven's door. St. Peter opens: "Nobody from McKinsey gets in here," he states categorically. "What do you mean, *in*?" asks the McKinsey man; "the place has to kick 5,000 *out*."

When people talk about efficiency, we quickly think of lay-offs. Rightly so: the number of jobs at large companies has declined continuously since the beginning of the 1980s. On the other hand, newly established firms and small and mid-sized companies are creating new jobs all the time.[96]

But efficiency is a more comprehensive principle than workplace rationalization. Inventors think about it; creativity is in demand; new products and processes can make sense – sometimes paradigm shifts are necessary to achieve substantial progress in productivity. All try to do their job with as little effort as possible. Even the moral philosopher Adam Smith saw a need to address this issue. He recognized the importance of the market and the division of labor as prerequisites for increased wealth, thus laying the foundation of modern economic theory. What I want to say is this: efficiency does not solely belong to management economics, but is a fundamental principle of the human will to create.

The words "*etwas unternehmen*" (to undertake something) sound very good in German. They promise initiative, achieving something that goes beyond daily routine; you hope for something exciting, enriching. The noun "*Unternehmen*" (company, enterprise) doesn't have quite as positive a connotation. The term "*Unternehmer*" (businessman, industrialist) elicits other images that tend to present those individuals in a negative light. In continental Europe, entrepreneurial activities are still tainted by negative connotations. So people will say: is entrepreneurship, i.e. the profit motive, a model for societal change? Profit is supposed to be a positive objective? In this view, my salary as a professor, paid by the state, is earned respectably; however, the fact that the Tea Campaign earns a profit is suspicious. When that little company, housed in the damp basement of the Free University's Institute for Economics Education, for which incidentally we paid a hefty rent, turned its first profit, a piece of news we proudly shared, the Department Administration cancelled our lease overnight. It was as if they had discovered a brothel in their basement.

Civil servants have always enjoyed greater prestige than merchants or tradesmen in Germany, where distain for the profit motive has long been a staple of social criticism. Don't all profits result from the exploitation of labor? Marx may be out, but the images of Early Capitalism have left an indelible imprint on our consciousness. While economists recognize profit as a mark of achievement (keeping costs lower than gross revenue), others see in it the triumph of the profit motive. A motive that defines, in the words of the philosopher Sloterdijk, the "class of entrepreneurs and holders of capital as those with devastating progressive energy smashing all stable relationships and blotting out all established conditions."[97]

9.9 Active Participation in Market Activities: The Case for Economic Enlightenment

Even if we want to say it less dramatically: it is a fact that economics not only penetrates more and more aspects of our lives, but that it is also starting to impact our everyday lives more than religion, culture or education. But before we speak of "unfettered capitalism" or start crusading against globalization, we should ask ourselves whether it is inevitable that we must yield the field of economic creativity to Sloterdijk's "class of entrepreneurs and owners of capital," that is, to *others*. We are already participating *passively* in the market – we compare prices and we compare the quality of products, assessed by a variety of professional consumer organizations. Many of us also pay attention to how we invest our savings, critically assessing the services of financial institutions. We know there is value in acting as informed and self-confident consumers.

Participating more *actively* in the market as suppliers of goods or services still looks like an unrealistic prospect to many of us – but perhaps only because we've not familiarized ourselves sufficiently with the opportunities and conditions in this field of activity.

The market system depends on participation. In this respect it is like the political system. Democracy depends on the competition between the parties and their political programs, while the market thrives on the competition of ideas and concepts in the economic arena. With regard to democracy, it's clear to us that we must be involved and give voice our own interests. Those who leave these matters to others shouldn't be surprised when no one pays attention to their concerns. But when it comes to the market, many of us allow ourselves the luxury of leaving it to others. To be sure, the market doesn't function perfectly. But democracy also doesn't function perfectly, yet nobody says we should ignore it, much less do away with it.

In the political system, the transition from monarchy and oligarchy to democracy took place during centuries past, whereas in the economic system the transition to greater participation, already taken for granted in the political sphere, still remains to be completed. Represented in the minds of the public largely by big companies and multinational concerns, the structures of the economic sphere still seem inaccessible. How can individuals become active participants in the economy, other than as employees, savers, or consumers?

Cynical interpretations of the market are widespread. But such views overlook its emancipatory potential. Market principles can be directed against the powerful. These principles did enforce participation by non-privileged social groups against feudalism and protectionism, and against royal trade privileges. Participation in economic activity was often the prerequisite for demanding political participation.

The economic emancipation of the individual is an important aspect of civic emancipation. "An empty sack cannot stand upright," wrote Benjamin Franklin, author, politician and Founding Father of the United States, in his *Poor Richard's Almanac* in 1740. Only when we are active agents of our economic condition, he meant to say, do we have the means and the motive to engage in civic participation for the greater good.

When in 1784 the German philosopher Immanuel Kant answered the question, "What is Enlightenment?" he gave a definition that related not only to man's political emancipation, but also to his economic self-liberation. According to the philosopher, "Enlightenment is man's emergence from his self-imposed immaturity." "Immaturity is the inability to use one's intelligence without guidance from another. This immaturity is self-imposed when its cause lies not in lack of understanding, but in lack of resolve and courage to use it without guidance from another." "Have courage to use your own understanding!" is the challenge that Kant issues.

The time has come. Today, entrepreneurial activity is an option for many more people than in the past. It is up to us to take advantage of this opportunity. Only then will we live up to a key promise of the Enlightenment – giving people voice and power in the economic sphere as well, giving them self-assurance and courage to strive for economic self-realization. Let's imagine a society in which economic decision-making is not determined by the power of the few, but by the power of ideas and by people no longer willing to leave the economic sphere to those who already control it.

10 Say Goodbye to Old Ways of Thinking (don't draw conclusions about the future based on the past)

Innovative start-ups are the engine for modern economies. They bring new technologies, new ideas and new concepts to the market, they maintain competitiveness, and they lead to increased productivity. On this, economic experts agree.

The developed Western industrial countries and Japan are islands of affluence with a sense of entitlement that seems grotesque when measured against global benchmarks. This observation, too, is not meant to be moralizing, but is rather intended to sharpen the focus of the eye accustomed to a Western perspective. As we compete with the entire world and as the countries once belittled as "developing countries" increasingly prove to be competitive, we must face up to this global perspective and challenge. The most modern factories are no longer being built in this country as was the case in post-war Germany; instead, they are being built in the up-and-coming newly industrialized countries. Today these countries offer precisely those features that once resulted in the *Wirtschaftswunder*, Germany's post-war economic miracle: low wages measured on a global scale, undervalued currencies and modern industrial facilities.

We're going to have to come up with some new ideas if we don't want to stand on the sidelines bemoaning the disruptions that globalization is causing here at home. Not all the developments are negative for us. In a post-industrial society, ideas and concepts play a vastly greater role than in the past. But with this insight we also have to change our attitudes. Why are so many people in this country competing for the last jobs in a society with a declining industrial base? Why are so few start-up entrepreneurs responding to this with ideas and concepts of their own? Why are we putting so little thought into what useful goods and services people will need in the future, both in our country and around the world?

10.1 What's to Be Done When the Economic Foundation Crumbles? (The example of Manaus, Brazil)

After the discovery of the vulcanization process in the second half of the 19th century, the Amazon region enjoyed a rubber boom that made Manaus one of the wealthiest cities in the world.

When Manaus opened its Teatro Amazonas with a performance of La Gioconda by Amilcare Ponchielli on January 7, 1897, even the paving stones around the opera house were made from a special mixture of sand and rubber so performances wouldn't be disturbed by passing horse-drawn carriages. A considerable share of the building material for the opera house was imported from Europe, and Manaus was the second city in the world to have public streetlights. Many of the city's citizens were extremely wealthy and lived in palaces. It wasn't uncommon to pack your dirty laundry into crates to be sent to Lisbon so it could be washed in clean Portuguese water and then shipped back to Manaus. The city's riches seemed to be virtually boundless and to stand on a solid foundation. Rubber production was going well and was constantly expanding.

The year 1915 brought the news that German chemists had succeeded in producing rubber synthetically. As a consequence, the price for natural rubber plummeted overnight. A few years later, Manaus was a deserted city whose mansions and palaces were falling into ruin.

What actually happened in Manaus following the news that its prior economic basis had crumbled? Did citizens react in a predictably conventional manner: protesting loudly about drastic cost-saving measures? Stating their outrage that public servants were fired en masse? Furious that buildings were left to ruin? Fighting to keep their opera?

Or were there voices saying something along the lines of: we're in a totally new situation; let's look ahead? Apparently not. (It was only in the 1990s that the development of tourism brought Manaus new sources of income that promise new development and perhaps even affluence.)

Are there circumstances under which an entire region has to be adapted to a new, and as yet untried, economic perspective? How did people react at the time? Can we learn something from their situation back then? In the case of Manaus, no adjustments were made, leading to a decades-long impoverishment of broad segments of the population. One thing, however, is certain: the people who just complained about the impoverishment and resulting devastation did little to improve the situation.

> Most of the time, the customary is even more inhibiting than the repressive.
>
> ERNST BLOCH

This example should be helpful in breaking free from a backwards-looking way of viewing things. Before its collapse Manaus believed itself secure, a center of economic power. Today in Germany many people, like those citizens of Manaus, still believe we are living at the center of the world's economic activity – or at least that we still have a chance to get back there.

By now, after the decline of its old industries, many other wage-intensive economic sectors in Germany are also slipping into hazardous straits. It is simply impossible to sweep under the rug a wage differential of one-to-seven as compared to Eastern Europe and of one-to-twenty in India and China.

Over the long run Germany's higher productivity cannot offset the difference in wage levels. On the contrary. When new state-of-the-art factories are built in the newly industrialized countries, the result is a huge jump in productivity there, and the infrastructure will also catch up by leaps and bounds

There is also no guarantee that areas like research and development will remain here with us in the First World. The graduates of universities in India and China are not inferior to our own, but are certainly much cheaper to hire, as seen from our own perspective. This book is not the place for conducting a discussion of Germany's future economic prospects. But it's getting hard to justify the irrational certainty that because everything is so bad already, things can only get better again. There is much to suggest that the descent from the first class of industrialized nations has only just begun.

A journalist colleague of mine and a neighbor, each employed by a (different) major publisher, recently told me very similar stories of how this decline, although still subtle, is proceeding much more rapidly than anticipated. First, the publishers failed to achieve their expected operating goals, so operations were streamlined and savings made at the expense of quality. In a second step, margins declined and subscriptions dwindled alarmingly – but the generally poor state of the economy was used to explain the situation. Now, services that were formerly central to the enterprise have been outsourced, and service providers are being squeezed for even lower prices.

The following year, the first wave of lay-offs occurs, and the publishers are pondering how they might win back their customers through new products and modern marketing concepts. Market research has shown that young target groups tend to be more online-savvy. A few bloggers are quickly hired to cultivate online communities, and all content is also put online. Genuine measures to change direction are being introduced late or not at all. The simple fact that fewer and fewer people are getting their information through print media is being glossed over through the introduction of more and more products, which rarely survive past their third issue. Everything is getting faster, shorter, more colorful and cheaper – an adaption to the Internet which, however, is still not recognized as genuine competition.

In the meantime competitors on the World Wide Web are working at a fraction of the costs. Perhaps they are smarter, younger and faster, and perhaps many people prefer to read a subjective blog and its commentary rather than a balanced expert article. Besides, this way they get every piece of news in real time and unfiltered through the RSS feed on their computers. This means I can all get my own newspapers on my own computer, laptop, tablet or cell phone, on precisely those topics that interest me.

What readers also like is that this costs much less, that forests don't have to be sacrificed for newsprint, and that there are no more newspapers to be recycled. In short, a customized electronic newspaper is economically and ecologically more rational than the traditional print product. Any major publisher that continues to publish a paper the way it always has been, increasing its subscription bonuses and running large print ads, may be heading even faster into the abyss.

You don't believe this? You say you still like to read your newspaper with your morning coffee, you are more of a tactile personality and will never cancel your newspaper subscription? Then maybe over the long run, you're a member of a dying breed. Perhaps the first passengers who rode the train from Nuremberg to Fuerth in 1835 also missed the jolting of the stagecoach, and it's been reported that they considered the speed of the "Adler" locomotive breathtakingly fast at more than 30 kilometers per hour.

By the way, both of my acquaintances are working in online ventures now.

Today, complaints and nostalgia help us as little as they did in the past. Laments about high unemployment and austerity measures don't get us anywhere. Only one thing is called for, and that's to look the new reality straight in the eye.

The question then has to be: is there a chance to reposition the economy? Where are these opportunities?[98] And of *whom* can we expect to recognize these opportunities?

Unfortunately, our political system struggles to maintain the status quo rather than prepare people for a new reality. Any company that openly transfers jobs abroad provokes politicians, stirs up the unions and creates negative publicity. The opposite course of action can be seen in a newly industrialized country like Thailand: it encourages its companies to outsource their production to China early enough and to seek out more profitable business segments before entire industries go bankrupt. And this when the wage differential between those two countries is less than 50%. In Germany the topic of "outsourcing" is taboo. These days, anyone who approaches economic problems from a Eurocentric perspective is rewarded, and anyone who demands radical rethinking is punished.

And an especially sharp rallying cry has been, "Our own pessimism is at fault." We don't have any gumption; we see things too negatively. The mere hint of a boomlet in the second half of 2007 was enough to trigger the old reflexes. What shall we do with the unexpected tax revenue? Isn't everything back on track? Recent worries: a ghost that just needs to be shooed away?

10.2 We Need Innovative Start-ups ...

In its country report on Germany 2005 the Global Entrepreneurship Monitor (GEM) points out the following: innovative start-ups stimulate competition, accelerate structural change and, if successful, generate growth and jobs. For a highly industrialized country like Germany, with few natural resources, they are the key variable for international competitiveness. Consequently Germany must intensify its efforts to increase innovation, in particular to foster innovative start-ups, especially in knowledge-intensive sectors.

In economics, as in economic policy, there is consensus that the establishment of new enterprises results in positive growth and increased employment. This, however, doesn't apply to *imitative* start-ups. Because they stimulate competition, they merely ensure that the markets don't stagnate, but as a rule they don't have much impact on employment.[99] *Innovative* start-ups, on the other hand, grow more rapidly than imitative start-ups because they create jobs, not only at these enterprises, but also at other companies such as suppliers, complementary vendors and service companies that recognize the new opportunities.[100]

10.3 … but they don't have to be hi-tech

In political discourse, but often even in the academic literature, the term "innovative start-up" is used almost exclusively to refer to technologically oriented start-ups. Other start-ups are ignored, even those presented here as concept-creative, which have the potential for the very same gains in productivity.

It's understandable that we have a tendency to see our economic future in the hi-tech areas because Germany has long drawn its economic power from its industrial strength. It's well known that even up until the 1970s the Federal Republic of Germany was a world leader in many technological areas, including mining, steel, shipbuilding, precision engineering, optics, the chemical, electronics and automotive industries, mechanical engineering and plant construction, just to mention some of the most familiar.

These days there are many competent industrial research and development centers throughout the world, not just in Central Europe, the USA and Japan, and all of them are in intense competition with each another. Relying exclusively on hi-tech is like investing all of your country's athletic resources in a single sport, overlooking the fact that you could perhaps earn medals more easily in other areas because there's less competition there.

And there is another aspect to consider: those who achieve research success are not necessarily the same people who can succeed as entrepreneurs. Transforming hi-tech into outstanding entrepreneurial performance is, as we have already seen, an entirely different discipline.[101]

In the meantime the growth markets in the globalizing world have moved to other fields, while we Germans still cling to images and notions of an industrialized society that are increasingly unrealistic. Tourism is a field we should perhaps consider. It‘s now the largest economic sector worldwide, with stable growth rates that won't change as quickly as those in other industries. Growing incomes and higher levels of education are leading to a disproportionately high demand in this area. If you hold up the quick obsolescence of, and intense competition between, hi-tech products against other economic areas, such as tourism, the (economic) choice shouldn't be difficult.[102] Asians have long recognized that the earth's temperate zones – and not the tropics – are the most pleasant places to be in, and word of this will spread even here. As will the fact that it isn't only sun, sand and sex that make tourism appealing, but that lifestyle, art and culture can also be highly attractive.

Germany's high standards of quality and credibility are solid, stable long-term competitive advantages. But in addition to the functionality and durability of German products, we can also introduce *new* standards of quality. In Germany we have made a good name for ourselves in matters of ecological innovation, product safety standards and foodstuff residue analysis. This is an update, if you will, of the "Made in Germany" standard that is still so highly regarded in other parts of the world.

To avoid misunderstanding: I'm not against hi-tech; I'm only against narrowing the field of vision to a single, highly competitive, high-risk sector of the economy that is characterized by rapid obsolescence.

It should also be mentioned that the government's faith in the wisdom of its choices is not borne out by their actual economic success. The authorities in charge of such measures believe they are able to identify which industrial developments have a promising future. For example, areas such as mainframe computers, atomic energy and Antarctic krill were at one point deemed especially promising for Germany and were heavily subsidized.[103] None of these policies brought success. People with an entrepreneurial bent have always been amazed that German life-time civil servants, of all people, are expected to have a good nose for ferreting out promising entrepreneurial projects for the country.

As spectacular as hi-tech start-ups are when they are successful, it is extremely difficult in the high-tech field for an individual founder or team to start a company and survive. Today technical progress proceeds at a much faster pace than in the past. In order to keep up with state-of-the-art research and development, as we described above, the entrepreneur must have connections with research institutions worldwide. What appears to be affordable for a few well-situated companies and university institutes is virtually impossible for most business founders who are not as well connected. If we want to win more people for a "culture of entrepreneurship," limiting our reach to hi-tech is much too narrow.

Statistically, too, successful hi-tech start-ups play a much smaller role than media reports would have us believe.
So let's not place all our bets on hi-tech development, but instead take the *application* of hi-tech as our starting point. Skype and ebuero are excellent examples of this.[104] Concept-creative start-ups are a perfect fit with innovative applications of hi-tech.

10.4 Igniting the First Spark in the "Idea Space" – Cultural Entrepreneurship

It's well known that the economic importance of the "Cultural Creatives" is growing. This is also reflected in the acceptance of terms such as "creative industries" and "creative economy." In the *post*industrial age societal values have long been shifting from basic needs to cultural values, and this also shows up in customer demand. But the fact that there's also an intimate relationship between entrepreneurship and the cultural-creative domain still seems strange to many Germans, who regard art and culture as a luxury, while economic activity is considered a necessity. Perhaps this helps us understand why in Germany entrepreneurship can still be equated with "business administration for founders."

We've already explained that in today's world the entrepreneur is more like an artist than a manager. The arguments made by Stanley Gryskiewicz and Frans Johansson also run along these same lines.[105]

Stanley Gryskiewicz of the Center for Creative Leadership recommends that we engage with art because it challenges us to find new perspectives; it touches us emotionally and makes us question the things we accept as self-evident.[106] He speaks of "positive turbulence" – a concept evoking Schumpeter's "creative destruction" – as an enriching stimulus for ideas, creating an atmosphere that liberates thinking from the limits of the status quo. It has four essential characteristics:

- "Welcoming difference" – allowing information and methods that are either unknown or unexpected, but which challenge our own approaches.
- "Inviting multiple perspectives" – encouraging divergent perspectives and unorthodox interpretations.
- "Controlling the intensity of turbulence" – moderating the scope and speed of change so that the desired processes do not change course and become negative.

- "Developing receptivity" – creating the necessary preconditions so that we can deal with changes and help shape them.

Frans Johansson, author and entrepreneur, argues that crucial impulses and innovations arise out of the interface of ideas from different cultures and disciplines. *Diversity drives innovation.* In such an "idea space," to use Johansson's term, you create the spark to ignite extraordinary developments and ways of looking at things. The author calls this the "Medici effect" after the famous banker dynasty of the Italian Renaissance.[107]

The Medici family supported and financed creative work across the entire spectrum. Thanks to the climate they created in Florence, sculptors, scientists, poets, philosophers, painters, financiers and architects learned from each other and moved beyond the limits of their own disciplines and cultures. In this way they created the world of new ideas that is known to us today as the Renaissance.[108]

But we don't have to look to Florence of the 15th and 16th centuries. Our own era contains similar elements. Cultural-creative skills are playing an ever-larger role in the economic success of start-ups. In his studies Karl Vesper points out that the concept-development phase is analogous to the artistic-creative process.[109]

> "The development of an entrepreneurial idea is,
> above all, a creative process.
> Its engineering is comparable
> to an artistic creative act."
>
> KARL VESPER

Cities like New York, Barcelona and Berlin have long enjoyed a scientific and cultural scene that does not lag behind that of Renaissance Florence. What the Medici seem to have accomplished was building bridges, creating an atmosphere in which there was an open invitation to "look over my shoulder" rather than an anxious emphasis on differences:[110] an idea space in which *cultural entrepreneurship* emerges.

So do we have to wait until a new culture of entrepreneurial activity develops on its own? A culture of entrepreneurship that draws much of its impetus from the creative arts? From people who craft ideas that cause "creative destruction" in the Schumpeterian sense, transforming an economy still dwelling on the accomplishments of the past, rather than the demands of the future? An economy that up to now has kept most people in the role of passive participants, rather than active shapers?

We will wait in vain for such a culture as long as we cling to obsolete ideas and an image of the entrepreneur that is off-putting rather than inviting. We can and must frame entrepreneurship as an open and attractive field for independent, creative action.

Economics is something much too important
for us to leave it to the economists.

(In the original: "War is much too important to leave to the military." The quotation is ascribed to Otto von Bismarck but probably goes back to Talleyrand. The economist Georg Simmel, known for his monetary theory, is said to have used the quotation in this way.)

How boring the world of architecture would be if there were only structural engineers. Only rarely would we get to see new conceptions and extravagant designs; from this perspective unusual aesthetic and functional designs could easily be regarded as foolish and unnecessary.

We mustn't leave the world of economics to business administrators and managers. They're the structural engineers – necessary, yes, even indispensible, but not inclined to develop new concepts or ideas that are experimental, different or provocative. And yet it is precisely these qualities that we need if we are to find new solutions for our times, for the problems we're facing.

Aren't we being unfair to the many business administrators who are doing their best to solve problems responsibly and with an eye to the future? Probably. But the point here is: *administration* in the sense of maintaining order, as mastery of complexity, privileges certain points of view that may *not exactly* be innovation-friendly, so we should not wait for new, experimental or avant-garde ideas to come from administrators.

10.5 Does our Educational System Teach for Entrepreneurship?

In the real world of the market, decisions are always made under conditions of uncertainty. School, however, is a system of certainty. The material is preselected, published in textbooks. The teachers know the exercises, the approaches for solving the problems and the solutions themselves. Complex reality is didactically reduced and assigned to particular subjects. Thus the setting of the educational system is at odds with the demands of entrepreneurship.

The current educational system is the problem, not the solution.

The setting in our educational institutions is counterproductive.

- In the real world decisions are made under conditions of uncertainty, not within a safe and secure framework
- You have to search for solutions; they're not just waiting to be found.
- Develop an economic future instead of teaching school subjects.
- Can entrepreneurship be taught by civil servants with lifetime tenure?
- Even the PISA study does not address the challenges of entrepreneurship.

These days learning processes are largely regimented, in content as well as in form. Graduation and the route to it, *i.e.*, the certificates or academic credits, are what really counts. Experts know that the model for professional qualification, the one the educational system knows and teaches – what qualifications will be in demand later in professional life – hasn't been valid for quite some time, but this is brushed aside in the course of daily school routines.

Are teachers training children to be little entrepreneurs? Are they promoting passion and the dogged pursuit of unusual ideas? Probably not very much. This would distract from the syllabus, from the lesson plans to be covered, from good grades and from much more.

Does the search for an economic future ever take place in school? You can argue that there's some connection between what's taught in school and the world of later life, that the classification scheme intrinsic to the subject and its structure doesn't always permit application to real-life situations, that overall the schools somehow do manage to function with a view toward future life prospects.

But be careful: as a rule these prospects involve finding a job and then working in it, which translates to *dependent* employment – that is, working for someone else.

In the past the educational system was able limit itself to this task. It was an employment system that was expected to generate new jobs. There was a kind of tacit division of labor that allocated the task of qualification to the educational system while the employment system was assigned the role of providing jobs, sorted according to profession. However, this division of labor is no longer functional.

Today we must insist that the educational system place graduates in a position to create their own jobs, or better yet, to create new jobs by establishing new companies.[111] However, if you examine the school setting and many teachers' attitudes on the subject of the market, not even taking into account that the world of private enterprise is totally foreign to most of those in the teaching profession, then you're forced to come to the conclusion that the educational system represents part of the problem rather than the solution.

Nonetheless the opportunities to make a contribution to entrepreneurship are not bad at all. The educational system always has fundamental advantages over the employment system when it comes down to knowledge, room for development and brainstorming. This is especially true when you compare it to life in the workaday world with its narrow constraints and time pressures. New ideas need places where it's possible to have openness, fresh approaches and experimentation. Recognizing and promoting the individual's specific capabilities, recognizing and accepting idiosyncrasies have actually long been the concern of sound pedagogical theory.

There is yet another reason why entrepreneurship occurs so rarely in the schools. There are a fair number of teachers who think, "*We really don't want to raise money-hungry little monsters.*" This is reminiscent of how some things were handled in the past in convent schools and then later in the public schools. Sexuality was blanked out – after all, we don't want to produce sex-obsessed little monsters. That meant keeping the subject of sex far away from children's innocent souls for as long as possible. Then later, when this position was no longer tenable because realistic pedagogues recognized that their charges' preoccupation with this topic would otherwise be uncontrolled and take place under a negative cloud, they invented sex education classes to teach them "the facts of life." But to begin with, the subject matter was structured so that it was rather a scary deterrent, not taking into account the young people's feelings and interests. Sexually transmitted diseases were presented in detail, long before AIDS gave this topic a whole other dimension.

From this, we could draw the conclusion that we need to teach students the economic "facts of life." But not to turn students off with the prospect of bookkeeping, accounting and balance sheets, but instead in a school that doesn't withhold the world of money and the market from us, a school that doesn't conceal its fascination and temptations. A school, which through both its content and setting familiarizes us with the opportunities for our own entrepreneurship.

The curiosity about economics and the ability for unconventional thinking exists. It has always existed, though buried by an educational system that trains for dependence in the form of paid work in the employ of others and by an anti-economic and anti-entrepreneurial attitude historically cultivated by a not inconsiderable number of pedagogues.

10.6 Has our Entrepreneurial Spirit Emigrated?

And what about the entrepreneurial spirit? With the emergence of the "investor" (in place of the entrepreneur), the emergence of "industrial policy" (instead of market forces) and the government favoring of "national champions" (instead of enforcing antitrust law), our entrepreneurial spirit seems to be in the process of dying out. For quite some time now the threat of mass lay-offs by the major players has succeeded in extorting desired policies from the government. The ugly motto of "privatize the profits and socialize the losses" has begun to catch on among the public. For the little guys the risk remains as high as before – extremely high, in fact. Most of them are gone within five years of start-up.

At the big German companies there are whole departments busily filling out applications for subsidies under programs administered by departments of the various EU ministries in Brussels. Has the German economy lost its entrepreneurial spirit?

Is it possible that in the meantime we're finding more initiative and willingness to take risks at Greenpeace, Transparency International, Foodwatch and other like-minded groups than we see in parts of corporate Germany? The increasingly prevalent idea that we must have national or EU champions in need of government direction and support does suggest this. Apparently these companies are incapable when left to their own devices and can only be made fit for international competition with the crutch of subsidies.

But isn't Germany famous for its entrepreneurially minded small and medium-sized companies? Names like Hasso Plattner, Hans Peter Stihl, Erich Sixt, Heinrich Deichmann, Hermann Kronseder, Heinz Dürr, Götz Werner and Claus Hipp come to mind.

Yes, Germany has outstanding entrepreneurial personalities, but how many are there? A few dozen? A few hundred? And are they representative of what we call the German economy? And finally, don't they all belong to a slightly older generation, which, in terms of the values they hold, seems to be dying out? People who don't indiscriminately throw around the money they've earned with their companies, people who don't go in for conspicuous consumption, but instead prefer to put their money back into their companies?

Now, some of our politicians are displaying strange symptoms: the entrepreneurial spirit seems to have taken them over. According to the beliefs of the Lahu Tribe in northern Thailand, ghosts like to seek out human bodies so that they can then act through them. Is this what has happened to these policitians? They are talking persuasively about fresh ideas, willingness to take on risks, and business founders who get their start in garages. The reality, of course, is very different. German workplace safety regulations have completely done away with those garage start-ups. Permanently. Holger Johnson's shelves and room dividers made of empty tea crates – simple, functional and free – didn't have a chance. Away with them! Arrange a discussion between a start-up entrepreneur and the bureaucrats of the regional authority? Forget about it.

So what about the fresh ideas? The ones that you – nicely dressed in your best suit and tie, of course – will present to your banker? Or to your start-up consultant, paid from public funds but probably without any business start-up experience of his own, who will enthusiastically take in the creative aspects of your idea concept – then carry it down to the business administration kitchen where the dish will be cooked up. Oh, get real; drop those crazy notions. A sympathetic smile for your eccentric ideas. Like that of a doctor for the patient he is trying to get to face reality.

It seems that the prevailing political belief in Continental Europe is that entrepreneurship has to be fostered with subsidies. It's not easy to comprehend how *subsidizing* entrepreneurship is supposed to stimulate the entrepreneurial spirit. But this is a view widely held by the politicians. Because the entrepreneurial spirit by its very essence means earning a profit *through one's own efforts*, subsidizing it is just as absurd as deciding to train a marathon runner by carrying him along the course on a stretcher, which might make him familiar with the total distance....

It would be interesting to see the outcome of an honest and unbiased, academically rigorous study of the true effects of our current subsidy policy.

On the subject of subsidies, this is what we hear from government administrators in charge of economic policy (and this is a direct quote): "We subsidize everything after all, so why not start-up entrepreneurs too!" Apparently they believe the lid of the coffin will open up only if they wave a lot of money over it.

Anyone who sees how much bureaucratic effort these incentives actually entail will recognize that they distract founders from their real task, *i.e.*, developing a convincing entrepreneurial design.

When funding was first offered for entrepreneurship projects, the small group of eight Berlin university professors, who had for years devoted themselves to the subject and who could point to successful start-ups in their immediate environment, suddenly grew to about 90. We worked for weeks and months on a large joint research and practice project that required a huge amount of effort for coordination and numerous compromises in its conception. Ultimately the project was rejected, and overnight the group was down to eight again. The spooky rush was over.

It is not that entrepreneurial spirit has to be brought from the government ministries to the universities, but exactly the opposite. We need a culture of entrepreneurial thinking and action that also engages our government, making it function far more experimentally, efficiently and less imperiously. We have to make the entrepreneurial field more attractive, and distance it from the practice of management and administrative thinking. We have to move it more in the direction of ideas, desires and passions. We need a *culture of entrepreneurship*, but this will not be created by bureaucracy with the enticement of a free lunch of subsidies served with a muddle of guidelines on the side.

What would really help? Exempting start-up entrepreneurs from bureaucratic requirements. For once, people should be given the chance to experiment entrepreneurially for a limited period of time. Much could be achieved if government were to give start-ups one year of freedom from bureaucracy, instead of babbling on endlessly about garage start-ups.[112]

10.7 Declaration of Independence

Entrepreneurship must liberate itself from the clutches of business administration. The hour of independence has struck.

Allan Gibb, an outstanding personality in the field of start-up research in Great Britain, goes so far as to urge that entrepreneurship be completely liberated from what he calls the *business knowledge context*. The significance of an intensive engagement with the concept has been pushed aside by the domineering transmission of business administration knowledge. It's necessary, says Gibb, to rescue entrepreneurship from this marginalization and to discard its customarily close connection with business administration because this is a much too restrictive pattern of thinking.[113]

Declaration of Independence

We no longer acknowledge the primacy of business administration.

We will use our financial resources frugally and rationally in our own best interest.

We recognize business administration as a welcome partner that supports us in the realization of our goals.

Our conventions were the stumbling block. The enemy was us. We were standing in our own way. We lived against a background of images from yesterday and the day before and clung to them stubbornly. This was understandable, perhaps even endearing, but it held us back unnecessarily. Today we're no longer able to work out all the details for the ideas and structures we work with.

When we hammer a nail into the wall, we don't need to know what alloy the hammerhead is made of, or how it's fastened to the wooden handle. But we should buy a high quality tool, not a piece of junk. Otherwise the hammerhead might go flying and hit us in the head. However, we don't need to take a course on hammer technology to distinguish quality from junk.

Independence doesn't mean that you now reject the previously dominant element in its entirety or that you denigrate it. It only means that you cast off its domination and show it its proper place. Business administration as a partner, yes. As the dominating authority, no.

11 An Invitation to a Dance

Jonas Ridderstråle & Kjell Nordström, two Swedish economists, gave their book *Funky Business* a German subtitle that translates into something like *How Smart Brains Get Capital to Dance*. [114] Their central thesis is that the new champions in economic life will be those who have ideas, even if they lack capital. The losers will be the capitalists with no ideas.

> Idea generators without capital will be the new champions, and capitalists without ideas will be left outside.
>
> RIDDERSTRÅLE & NORDSTRÖM

You may think you're not suited for entrepreneurship because you can't get excited about the world of money, and you also sense there's a bit of idealism in you? You weren't born to be a start-up entrepreneur because you're not pushy enough and lack the drive?

Combine your idealism and your commitment to a better society with the desire for a frugal, imaginative and creative use of resources.

Start by making a good, existing product cheaper. This isn't an insignificant assignment. It makes good economic sense to push for lower prices. We have scarcely any power to boost our wages and salaries because of the growing competition from the newly industrialized and developing countries. But in the case of our prices, which are high by global standards, there is room for some downward movement. Even with flat wages and salaries, falling prices would increase our prosperity. If we can cut the prices of foodstuffs and textiles – and the chances of accomplishing this are good –, this would have positive social consequences. Anyone with only a modest income spends a disproportionately high amount on these living expenses.

If you feel drawn to creative work, stick with it! Entrepreneurship *is* art. It's the creative challenge of a new concept that demands inspiration, intuition and sensitivity for social contexts. But anyone who seeks inspiration and intuition needs leisure, distance and a vision of the big picture, which the hectic pace of daily life doesn't allow. Don't try to become a business administrator. Instead, listen to him closely, as you would to the words of an attorney. He's working with the techniques you urgently need. But don't ever allow these means to become your ends, because that will divert you from your path to success. Rediscover your childlike curiosity and don't allow yourself to be overly impressed by conventional notions, even and especially in the field of economics. If you're able to do this, then you'll have a good chance of replacing boredom and busyness with something better. Keep working on your concept as long as necessary, until you yourself are completely convinced by it.

Entrepreneurship offers you the opportunity to work with unconventional ideas and perspectives, and then through them to participate successfully in economic life. A "culture of entrepreneurship" purposely includes artists, mavericks and people with a sense of social commitment, who in the past saw little opportunity to participate actively in the economic realm. Our society needs entrepreneurial initiatives that not only tease out new needs, but which respond to existing problems with economic, social and also artistic imagination.

There are three steps by which we can radically change the entrepreneurial landscape. Actually, they are only mental steps, viewing the problem from new angles, if you will, that will make it possible for us to approach the subject of starting a business from a very different perspective.

The first step is to recognize that today good concepts are more important than capital.

The next step is to apply the principle of the division of labor much more radically to the field of entrepreneurship. The notion that entrepreneurs must have relevant training in all areas of their business inevitably results in placing excessive demands on them.

The third step is to create a company from components. Division of labor and specialization open up the possibility of creating a company formed almost exclusively out of components. A newly-founded company like this operates professionally from Day 1, requires much less capital, reduces risk and is less susceptible to the typical crises that come with a company's growth.

Eliminating the entire burden of business administration clears the way for the business founder to concentrate on working on his entrepreneurial concept. When the artist doesn't have to build the frame, stretch the canvas and grind the pigments himself, he can focus on the creative act of painting and concentrate all his energies on this element.

> All the forces in the world are not so powerful as an idea whose time has come.
>
> VICTOR HUGO

Creating a company from a concept restores the marketplace as a competition of ideas. It re-invents economics as the most beautiful of all the arts: it enables imaginative creating fitted to one's time, place and person, opening up sustainable and enduring economic prospects. It is useful to society because it draws attention to itself through good and reasonably priced products. It is a way that doesn't increase inequities, but can lead to a more equitable distribution of income and wealth through broader participation in entrepreneurial activity.

"Entrepreneurship for the many" is at present still a vision – but a vision within our grasp.

Appendix

Everyone can become an entrepreneur Interview with Professor Muhammad Yunus (Excerpt)[115]

The inequitable distribution of income and wealth and the ever-widening gap between rich and poor are creating a socially explosive situation, a kind of time bomb that could explode at any time. Conventional policies that attempt to redistribute wealth, whether through progressive tax rates, wage policies, or through government or private sector aid programs, have all proven to be unsuitable or insufficient to arrest and reverse the trend towards greater economic disparity.

Muhammed Yunus, a professor of economics, has developed a program, which has earned respect throughout the world and been adapted in many countries. His program is to view the poor as potential entrepreneurs, and with the help of micro-loans put them in a position to operate their own micro-enterprises – and, as it turns out, with astounding success. That Yunus was awarded the Nobel *Peace* Prize for his life's work attests to the fact that this project is about much more than just improving the economic situation of those involved. Lasting peace will come only when a sustainable response to the problem of the wage and wealth disparity has been found.

Faltin: As economists we know that the cause or centre of unequal income distribution and unequal wealth distribution is due to commercial activity. That's where the problem starts. Those who are entrepreneurs usually accumulate a lot of money and others don't. So if you can increase participation in entrepreneurship that would be the decisive point to change society and all the inequality.

Yunus: Absolutely. My own feeling is all human beings can by birth become entrepreneurs. It's rooted in the person itself. But the society we have created doesn't allow most of the people to bring out the gift they carry inside of them. They don't know that they possess the entrepreneurial capability. They look at it in a way as "I don't know what to do. I work for you because I have nothing good to discover inside of me. That's the point where society goes wrong. Society should encourage everybody to explore the potential they have inside of them. It's a wonderful gift you have and never unwrapped, never looked at and that's why you don't know. That's where we're coming from in creating the problem of inequality because your own thinking has remained little. You have not seen that you're there. If you were aware of your capabilities, you could contribute those to the society.

Faltin: But nobody believes that. You say every body possesses the capability to engage in commercial activity, even the ones who are not highly educated and not in the hunting field. Can really everybody become an entrepreneur?

Yunus: Yes. Even the beggar woman or the beggar man in the streets of Bangladesh, India or Africa has as much entrepreneurial potential inside as anybody else in the world. They simply have never opened their box to find out that it's all in there because they never knew that it's there. Society never allowed, never facilitated unwrapping that gift. In terms of potential we are all equal. Some have discovered or caught a little of that potential, others haven't.

Faltin: What about the educational system. Usually we believe that the educational system has to equip people with the aforementioned capabilities and talents.

Yunus: Not only education I would say, rather appropriate education. Some education can give you a wrong mindset. Education can train and prepare yourself to work for somebody. That's not a good education as regards entrepreneurship. Education should aim at telling the following message to the people: "You could do things on your own". But if you want as an option to work for somebody else, that's OK, too. You can do it yourself, you have the capability. Education should also encourage you to think and find your own talents instead of only preparing you for the necessary steps to have a little job in a company. One shouldn't be prevented from finding out that one could have done something completely different. Education has to be at open ends so that you are aware of your opportunities. Information technology is very important in that regard as well. You have to be able to explore your own thing instead of only following what is in your textbooks and not what is beyond your textbooks. Information technology does not have a textbook so you have to design your own textbook, what you want to know about yourself, the world, what kind of thing you want to do yourself. Indeed, information technology today comes as a very powerful instrument to discover yourself.

Faltin: All the time we're busy in turning ourselves into entrepreneurs. What is your advice to us? Where should we start in order to become entrepreneurs in the Western culture?

Yunus: The starting point is only at the personal level and creating institutions, educational opportunities and websites, which can be contacted by the individual people to raise questions such as: "What am I doing here? I could have done this, I could have done that. Why don't we explore this one a little bit more?" It's about creating individuals to be themselves, discover themselves and explore themselves. That spirit of exploring oneself is the most important act. Of all the things we can do to help becoming entrepreneurs, this is the best thing we can all do.

When even Muslim women living under the most extreme social conditions in a severely underdeveloped country can successfully become entrepreneurs, we would expect that this is possible here in this country under infinitely more favorable conditions. Not just for the negligible number of people who have established businesses in this country up until now, but for as many people as possible.

Notes

1 Stefan Wagner, in *Red Bulletin*, June 2011.
2 http://blogs.forbes.com/danisenberg/2011/06/21/green-shoots-of-an-entrepreneurial-spring/ Economist, 6/16/11 http://ideas.economist.com/blog/start-revolution
3 The lively discussions triggered by this idea and the resulting establishment of the *Projektwerkstatt* company in 1985 are described in Faltin/Zimmer 1996, pp. 184 ff., p. 198 f.
4 The concept of "social entrepreneurship" is only in its infancy in Germany. The idea of thinking like an entrepreneur and at the same time acting out of social commitment (and not using this commitment solely as a PR measure) is still unusual in Germany. One is assigned to either one camp or the other.
5 Cf. Faltin/Zimmer 1996, pp. 161 ff.
6 Cf. Goebel 1990.
7 Under the prevailing view, starting a company is inconceivable without efforts to obtain financing, but it is especially inconceivable without an emphasis on the implementation of business administration practices. Only when you have successfully demonstrated the opposite in practice is there a chance that a new approach will be accepted.
8 Agora, the Greek word for marketplace, was the place for political discussions in ancient Athens.
9 *Süddeutsche Zeitung*, online edition, October 26, 2006.
10 *Spiegel online*, December 2, 2007.
11 In Chapter 7.3, "Compose your company," you will find the small company "Rapskernoel.info," which likewise originated in the shadow of the Tea Campaign.
12 The origin of the Swiss grocery chain Migros is described in detail in Faltin/Zimmer 1996, pp. 161 ff.
13 Cf. Gebhardt 1991.
14 The following description follows *Mission X: Der Kampf um die schwarze Formel* [Mission X: The Fight for the Black Formula].
15 *Gablers neues Wirtschaftslexikon* [Gabler's New Economic Lexikon] also concedes that there is no German equivalent for the internationally long-established concept of entrepreneurship.
16 For many: von Collrepp 2004.
17 This is normally undertaken by means of a business plan.
18 Cf. Timmons 1994.
19 The term *Geschäftsmodell* , a literal translation of the American term "business model," appears to be prevailing in the German language literature – a very unfortunate word coinage. It reduces the thinking required/required intellectual activity to the word "business" while the concept "model" sounds like theory even though the concept must be measured against its suitability to be executed in practice.

20 *Institut der Deutschen Wirtschaft*, Cologne 2006, "*Wachstumsfaktor Innovation.*"
21 Cf. Mitchell/Coles 2003, p. 19.
22 Cf. Goleman 1997.
23 Like kindergarten or zeitgeist the German word gestalt is a concept used internationally.
24 Cf. Menger 2006.
25 Szyperski (2004) also emphasizes the parallels between art and entrepreneurial activities.
26 Cf. Jacobson 2003.
27 Cf. Goebel 1990.
28 Cf. Jacobsen 2003.
29 Cf. Gratzon 2004, who describes how he developed a successful concept out of his proverbial hammock.
30 See for example the recent interest in strategy considerations based on the interplay between planning and high ability to improvise, as they were carried by the strategies of Scharnhorst or Gneisenau.
31 Cf. Jacobsen 2003.
32 Too bad that Hoof sold to the Otto Group. We will have to wait to see if the new owners continue the policy of the founders.
33 Cf. Birkenbach 2007.
34 Cf. Malik 2006, pp. 17 ff. and Birkenbach 2007, p. 212 f.
35 Cf. Malik 2006, p. 36.
36 "Leading" in the sense of thinking ahead, setting goals – everything that is expressed in the English term "leadership."
37 Ingvar Kamprad, founder of Ikea, has said about himself, "I am a disaster as an organizer."
38 Cf. Timmons 1994.
39 Szyperski also argues in favor of a separation. A good businessman requires an efficient manager.
40 Cf. Faltin 2001, p. 127 f.
41 *Die Zeit*, November 16, 2006, no. 47.
42 Roddick 1991
43 I still recalled with distaste such discussions from Germany. I remember one test particularly well. I wanted to go to Mozambique. After the Portuguese were replaced in 1976, a new type of school was to be established there, one that was supposed to combine both practice and theory before the backdrop of the country's enormous economic problems. My colleague Ludwig Gutschmid and I offered our assistance. We had already taken half a year of Portuguese classes, and now we still needed a visa. However, you could only obtain one if it was supported by the Akafrik Group, a solidarity committee for Africa in Bielefeld. Ludwig and I competed. A first-semester sociology student at the University of Bielefeld questioned us intensively about our objectives and motivation, and although we had studied the country, prepared conscientiously and were sympathetic to the anti-colonialists, neither of us passed this ideo-

logical test. The situation in Manila was not quite so dogmatic, but it was in essence similar.

44 Incidentally, you can offer this service yourself. In fact, for significantly less than 1,000 Euros you can install the technology, i.e. all the software and hardware, including the billing system, and even compete with Skype itself (www.outbox.de).

45 As we know, Skype was sold to eBay for more than US $ 1.8 billion (plus additional consideration). With more than 300 million users Skype is currently the largest telecommunications company in the world by far, and this at telephone rates that the telecommunication giants cannot match. Naturally we all think in conventional categories, and in the case of Skype we are amazed how such a small team was able to achieve such an increase in value in such a short period of time. If, on the other hand, you look at Skype from the standpoint of market performance and measure it against the valuations of established companies, the purchase price is not surprising.

46 In June 2009 the Federal Ministry for Economics and Technology honored the concept "Founding a company with components" as one of the four best ideas to increase the number and quality of sustainable start-ups in Germany.

47 The following statements are based on a university lecture on entrepreneurship by Professor Georg Schreyögg at the Free University of Berlin during the 2006 summer semester.

48 Cf. Fritsch/Weyh 2006.

49 Cf. Aldrich/Auster 1986.

50 Greiner 1998, p. 60, cited in a lecture on entrepreneurship by Professor Schreyögg at the Free University of Berlin during the 2006 summer semester.

51 Greiner 1998, p. 60, cited in a lecture on entrepreneurship by Professor Schreyögg at the Free University of Berlin during the 2006 summer semester.

52 Greiner 1998, p. 62, cited in a lecture on entrepreneurship by Professor Schreyögg at the Free University of Berlin during the 2006 summer semester.

53 Bygrave 1994.

54 There are already first steps in this direction, www.silber-zahnbuerste.de.

55 Even in the USA, the birthplace of venture capital and business angels, a good 70% of the capital necessary for start-ups come from family and friends.

56 I remember one student who had worked on the Tea Campaign and needed a recommendation from one of his professors for an application. He asked me *not* to mention his (extremely valuable) collaboration on the Tea Campaign because he thought this would be damaging to this career.

57 Cf. Suter 2002.

58 If you want more details, see Faltin/Zimmer 1996, p. 102 ff.

59 Cf. Goleman/Kaufman/Ray: 2002.
60 Cf. Flach 2003.
61 Cf. Kniess 2006.
62 The purchase and sale of foreign currencies, products or securities between two or more markets in order to earn a direct profit by exploiting the differences between the various market prices.
63 To be sure, on the Internet there are a number of examples where the lightning-fast takeover of functioning concepts from the US was successful. Alando/eBay was one of the first of these cases.
64 Cf. Kirzner 1978.
65 According to the June 1938 (!) issue of the publication *Scientific American* (quoted from *Die Welt*, November 28, 1992) anyone who has a radio or a telephone can receive a newspaper by fax with the help of a "device in a small box."
66 Cf. *The Nation*, August 7, 1995.
67 Cf. Ripsas/Zumholz/Kolata 2007.
68 Cf. Timmons 1994
69 Cf. Timmons/Spinelli/Zacharakis 2004.
70 Cf. Horx 2001, p. 146.
71 Ripsas/Zumholz/Kolata 2007, p. 2.
72 The interviews with the two founders Hinrichs and Dariani can be found at http://labor.entrepreneurship.de/blog/category/video/.
73 This seems to be the case even for the pharmaceutical industry, which maintains that it puts particularly large amounts of money into research. In his book *Kranke Geschäfte* [a book about the pharmaceutical industry], Markus Grill argues that twice as much money goes into marketing as is invested in research (Grill 2007, p. 15 ff.).
74 If you absolutely have to have a mission statement, download it free from Dilbert's (nonsense) mission statement generator on the Internet.
75 The "Ökonomie der Aufmerksamkeit" [*Economics of Attention*] (Franck 1998) is a newer, more scientific expression of this thought. In the struggle for success in the market, what is important is attracting the attention of the largest target group possible.
76 File no. 19620270.1, German Patent Office; supplemental application, January 20, 1997, File. No.19753179.2.
77 Gerald Hüther, *Was wir sind und was wir sein könnten. Nachdruck, S. Fischer Verlag, 2011* . If you do something with passion, new brain synapses and synaptic connections are generated, enhancing the potential of your brain.
78 Cf. Kawasaki 2004, p. 3.
79 Cf. op. cit., p. 5.
80 Cf. Branson 2002.
81 Jacobsen 2003, p. 42.
82 Cf. op. cit., p. 56.
83 Cf. Horx 2001.
84 Morgan 1991, p. 292.

85 Cf. the dissertation by Jacobsen 2003, pp. 54 ff., who has included virtually all of the available empirical studies in her research. Cf. also Ripsas 1997.
86 Cf. Jacobsen 2003, p. 72.
87 Cf. Ripsas 1997.
88 Cf. Jacobsen 2003, pp. 72ff.
89 Cf. Ripsas 1997.
90 Cf. Branson 2002.
91 Cf. Bergmann 2004.
92 Cf. Pinchot 1985. Pinchot introduced this concept into the discussion. He describes the employees of a company who function as entrepreneurs in this company even though they are only employees.
93 Cf. Faltin 2001, pp. 127 ff.
94 Cf. Casson 1990.
95 Cf. Schumpeter 1993.
96 Cf. Albach/Dahremöller 1986, p. 11.
97 Sloterdijk 2005, p. 100.
98 If there is no chance of this, do we have to think about an orderly, rather than otherwise catastrophic retreat? Must we resign ourselves to the possibility of rising mass unemployment, social unrest, and a sharp increase in criminality, prostitution and the other side effects of poverty?
99 Cf. Franke/Lüthje 2004, p. 38
100 Cf. op. cit., p. 39.
101 Remember Josef Schumpeter who made the distinction between "invention" and "innovation" the starting point for his analysis.
102 Perhaps Germany's future also lies in the preservation of its history, its intellectual life, art, culture and architectural monuments. What is true for Venice, Paris and the historic core of Amsterdam also applies on a smaller scale to the central core of many cities rich with historical tradition.
103 Especially in East Germany, there is an impressive list of government investments in failed development projects.
104 Both the Tea Campaign and ebuero integrate hi-tech into their processes to a very high degree. When a customer clicks "Okay" for his order on the Tea Campaign's webpage, the underlying software handles all the invoicing, bookkeeping and inventory management. At the same time, an address label is printed at the shipper's premises. Our software even programs the scanner on site at the packager's that reads the bar code on the package and verifies whether or not it corresponds to the order. Thus our online shop and most underlying processes are fully automated. We also offer this as a business component to other start-up entrepreneurs. I mention these details so that you can see how much this would simplify establishing your own business and make it much more economical than handling all these processes for yourself. Concept-creative start-ups go very well with innovative hi-tech applications.
105 Cf. Gryskiewicz 2006 and Johansson 2004.

106 Cf. Gryskiewicz 2006, pp. 21 ff.
107 Cf. Johansson 2004, p. 2.
108 Cf. ibid., p. 2.
109 Cf. Vesper 1993.
110 We should, however, ask to what extent the image we have of this banking family and their age has been glorified. After all, not all the Medici were model citizens.
111 Cf. Faltin 1998, p. 19.
112 The same way they used to promote home ownership: you were able to claim a special depreciation allowance once in your lifetime.
113 Cf. Gibb 2001.
114 Cf. Ridderstråle/Nordström 2000.
115 The interview was recorded at the Vision Summit 2007 in Berlin. The video can be watched at www.entrepreneurship.de/yunus

Bibliography

Albach, Horst/Dahremöller, Axel 1986: *Der Beitrag des Mittelstandes bei der Lösung von Beschäftigungsproblemen in der Bundesrepublik Deutschland*. IfM-Materialien Nr. 40, Institut für Mittelstandsforschung, Bonn

Aldrich, H. E./Auster, E. 1986: "Even Dwarfs Started Small: Liabilities of Size and Age and their Strategic Implications". In: *Research in Organizational Behaviour*, Bd. 8, S. 165–198

Ambrosch, Marcus 2010: *Effectuation – Unternehmergeist denkt anders!* Echomedia Verlag, Wien

Bendixen, Peter 2003: *Das verengte Weltbild der Ökonomie. Zeitgemäß Wirtschaften durch kulturelle Kompetenz*. Wissenschaftliche Buchgesellschaft, Darmstadt

Bergmann, Frithjof 2004: *Neue Arbeit, neue Kultur*. Arbor Verlag, Freiamt im Schwarzwald

Birkenbach, Katja 2007: *"Form follows Function" als ein Gestaltungsprinzip für das Geschäftsmodell eines Entrepreneurs*. Dissertation, Manuskript, Berlin

Blum, Ulrich/Leibbrand, Frank 2001: *Entrepreneurship und Unternehmertum. Denkstrukturen für eine neue Zeit*. Gabler Verlag, Wiesbaden

Branson, Richard 1999: Losing my Virginity. Crown Business

Bygrave, William D. 1994: "The Entrepreneurial Process". In: Bygrave, William D.: *The Portable MBA in Entrepreneurship*. Wiley, Hoboken, NJ

Casson, Marc (Hrsg.) 1990: *Entrepreneurship*. E. Elgar Pub., Brookfield, Vt.

Chan, Kim W./ Mauborgne, Renée 2005:*Blue Ocean Strategy: How to Create Uncontested Market Space and Make the Competition Irrelevant* Mcgraw-Hill Professional

Collrepp, Friedrich v. 2004: *Handbuch Existenzgründung: Für die ersten Schritte in die dauerhaft erfolgreiche Selbständigkeit*. 4. Aufl., Schäffer-Poeschel Verlag, Stuttgart

Curtis, Lee J. 1999: *Lloyd Loom. Wohnen mit klassischen Korbmöbeln*. Mosaik Verlag, München/ Curtis, Lee J. 1991 (re-issue): Lloyd Loom: *Woven Fibre Furniture*. Salamander Books

Dees, J. Gregory 2001: *The Meaning of "Social Entrepreneurship"*. Kauffman Centre for Entrepreneurial Leadership, Stanford

Dowling, Michael 2003: *Gründungsmanagement*. 2. Aufl., Springer Verlag, Berlin

Drucker, Peter F. 1985: *Innovation and Entrepreneurship*. HarperCollins, New York

Faltin, Guenter 1987: "Bildung und Einkommenserzielung. Das Defizit: Unternehmerische Qualifikation". In: Axt, Heinz-Jürgen (Hrsg.): *Ausbildungs- und Beschäftigungskrise in der Dritten Welt*. Verlag für Interkulturelle Kommunikation, Frankfurt am Main

Faltin, Guenter 1998: "Das Netz weiter werfen – Für eine neue Kultur unternehmerischen Handelns". In: Faltin, Guenter/Ripsas, Sven/Zimmer, Jürgen (Hrsg.): *Entrepreneurship. Wie aus Ideen Unternehmen werden.* C.H. Beck, München

Faltin, Guenter 2001: "Creating a Culture of Innovative Entrepreneurship". In: *Journal of International Business and Economy*, Vol. 2, No. 1, S. 123–140

Faltin, Guenter 2005: "Für eine Kultur des Unternehmerischen". In: Bucher, Anton/Lauermann, Karin/Walcher, Elisabeth: *Leistung – Lust & Last.* Obv & Hpt, Wien

Faltin, Guenter 2007: *Erfolgreich gründen. Der Unternehmer als Künstler und Komponist.* Deutscher Industrie- und Handelskammertag, Berlin

Faltin, Guenter/Zimmer, Jürgen 1996: *Reichtum von unten. Die neuen Chancen der Kleinen.* 2. Aufl., Aufbau Verlag, Berlin

Ferriss, Timothy 2007: *The 4-Hour Workweek.* Crown Publishers, New York

Fink, Klaus 2008: *Entrepreneurship. Theorie und Fallstudien zu Gründungs-, Wachstums- und KMU-Management.* facultas.wuv, Wien

Flach, Frederick F. 2003: *In der Krise kommt die Kraft.* Herder Verlag, Freiburg

Fleischmann, Fritz: *Entrepreneurship as emancipation: The history of an idea.* http://labor.entrepreneurship.de/tiki-index.php?page=Ressourcen

Franke, Nikolaus/Lüthje, Christian 2004: "Entrepreneurship und Innovation".In: Achleitner, Ann-Kristin et al. (Hrsg.): *Jahrbuch Entrepreneurship 2003/2004.* Springer-Verlag, Berlin

Friebe, Holm/Lobo Sascha 2006: *Wir nennen es Arbeit.* Heyne Verlag, München

Fritsch, Michael/Weyh, Antje 2006: "How Large are the Direct Employment Effects of New Businesses? – An Empirical Investigation". In: *Small Business Economics*, 27, S. 245-260

Fueglisthaler, Urs 2004: *Entrepreneurship.* Gabler Verlag, Wiesbaden

Gamper, Karl 2005: *So schön kann Wirtschaft sein.* J. Kamphausen Verlag, Bielefeld

Gamper, Jwala und Karl 2007: *Es ist alles gesagt. Jetzt braucht es Beispiele.* edition.gamper.com

Gebhardt, Eike 1991: *Abschied von der Autorität. Die Manager der Postmoderne.* Gabler Verlag, Wiesbaden

Gibb, Allan 1999: "Can we build effective Entrepreneurship through Management Development?" In: *Journal of General Management*, Vol. 24, No. 4

Gibb, Allan 2001:"Creative, Condusive Environments for Learning an Entrepreneurship. Living with, Dealing with, Creating and Enjoying Uncertainty and Complexity". Address to the Conference of the entrepreneurship Forum, Naples

Godin, Seth 2004: *Free Prize Inside!.* Penguin Group, New York

Goebel, Peter 1990: *Erfolgreiche Jungunternehmer.* Moderne Verlagsgesellschaft, München

Goleman, Daniel 1997: *Emotionale Intelligenz*. Deutscher Taschenbuch Verlag, München (Original: *Emotional Intelligence. Why it can matter more than IG*. Bantam Books, New York 1995)

Goleman, Daniel/Kaufman, Paul/Ray, Michael 2002: *Kreativität entdecken*. Carl Hanser Verlag, München

Gratzon, Fred 2004: *The Lazy Way To Success*. J. Kamphausen Verlag, Bielefeld / Gratzon, Fred 2003: *The Lazy Way To Success: How To Do Nothing and Accomplish Everything*. Soma Press

Greiner, Larry E. 1998: Commentary and Revision of HBR Classic, "Evolution and Revolution as Organizations Grow", *Harvard Business Review* 76 (3/1998), S. 55–68, Commentary "Revolution is still inevitable", S. 64–65

Grill, Markus 2007: *Kranke Geschäfte. Wie die Pharmaindustrie uns manipuliert*. Rowohlt, Reinbek bei Hamburg

Gryskiewicz, Stanley 2006: *Positive Turbulence, Developing Climates for Creativity, Innovation and Renewal*. Center for Creative Leadership, Greensboro, N.C.

Heinle, Thomas 2005: *Finde deinen Job*. Goldmann, München

Hemer, Joachim/Berteit, Herbert/Walter, Gerd/Göthner, Maximilian 2006: *Erfolgsfaktoren für Unternehmensausgründungen aus der Wissenschaft*. Studien zum deutschen Innovations system Nr. 05-2006, Herausgeber: BMBF, Berlin

Hansen, Klaus P. 1992: *Die Mentalität des Erwerbs: Erfolgsphilosophien amerikanischer Unternehmer*. Campus Verlag, Frankfurt am Main/ New York

Hinterhuber Hans H. 1992: *Strategische Unternehmensführung*. De Gruyter, Berlin/New York

Horx, Matthias 2001: *Smart Capitalism*. Eichborn Verlag, Frankfurt am Main

Horx, Matthias 2006: *How We Will Live. A Synthesis of Life in the Future*. Cyan Communications Ltd.

Hüther, Gerald 2011: *Was wir sind und was wir sein könnten*. Nachdruck, S. Fischer Verlag

Jacobsen, Liv Kirsten 2003: *Bestimmungsfaktoren für Erfolg im Entrepreneurship – Entwicklung eines umfassenden Modells*. Dissertation im Fachbereich Erziehungswissenschaft und Psychologie der Freien Universität Berlin, Berlin

Jarvis, Jeff 2009: What Would Google Do?. HarperBusiness

Johansson, Frans 2004: *The Medici Effect. Breakthrough insights at the intersection of ideas, concepts, and cultures*. Harvard Business School Press, Boston, Mass.

Kawasaki, Guy 2004: *The Art of The Start*. Penguin, New York

Kirzner, Israel M. 1978: *Competition and Entrepreneurship*. University of Chicago Press

Klandt, Heinz 1999: *Gründungsmanagement: Der integrierte Unternehmensplan*. Oldenbourg Verlag, München/Wien

Knieß, Michael 2006: *Kreativitätstechniken. Möglichkeiten und Übungen*. Beck in dtv, München

Kollmann, Tobias (Hrsg.): *Gabler Kompakt-Lexikon Unternehmensgründung 2005*. Gabler, Wiesbaden Literaturverzeichnis 245

Kulicke, Marianne/Görisch, Jens/Stahlecker, Thomas 2005: *Erfahrungen aus EXIST – Querschau über die einzelnen Projekte*. Fraunhofer-Institut für Systemtechnik und Innovationsforschung, Karlsruhe

Malek, Miroslaw/Ibach, Peter K. 2004: *Entrepreneurship: Prinzipien, Ideen und Geschäftsmodelle zur Unternehmensgründung im Informationszeitalter*. dpunkt.verlag, Heidelberg

Malik, Fredmund 2006: *Führen. Leisten. Leben*. 10. Auflage, Campus Verlag, Frankfurt am Main/New York

May, Matthew E./Kawasaki, Guy 2009: *In Pursuit of Elegance: Why the Best Ideas Have Something Missing*, Random House, New York

Mellewigt, T./Witt, P. 2002: "Die Bedeutung des Vorgründungsprozesses für die Evolution von Unternehmen: Stand der empirischen Forschung". In: *Zeitschrift für Betriebswirtschaft* 72, S. 81–110

Menger, Pierre-Michel 2006: *Kunst und Brot. Die Metamorphosen des Arbeitnehmers*. UvK Verlagsgesellschaft, Konstanz

Mitchell, Donald/Coles, Carol 2003: "The ultimate competitive advantage of continuing business model innovation", *The Journal of Business Strategy*, Vol. 24, S. 15–21

Moog, Petra 2005: *Good Practice in der Entrepreneurship-Ausbildung – Versuch eines internationalen Vergleichs*. Studie für den FGF, Bonn

Morgan, Gareth 1991: "Emerging Waves and Challenges: The Need for New Competencies and Mindsets". In: Henry, J. (Hrsg.): *Creative Management*. Sage Publications, London/Newbury Park/New Delhi

Opoczynski, Michael 2005: *ZDF WISO Ratgeber Existenzgründung: Business Plan/Finanzierung und Rechtsform /Steuern und Versicherungen/Checklisten und Adressen*. Redline Wirtschaft, Frankfurt am Main

Osterwalder, Alexander 2004: *The Business Model Ontology. A Proposition in a Design Science Approach*. Dissertation, vorgelegt in der Ecole des Hautes Etudes Commerciales de l'Université de Lausanne

Osterwalder, Alexander/ Pigneur, Yves 2010: Business Model Generation: A Handbook for Visionaries, Game Changers, and Challengers. John Wiley & Sons

Pinchot, Gifford 1985: *Intrapreneuring. Why you don't have to leave the corporation to become an entrepreneur*. Harper & Row, New York

Reitmeyer, Dieter (mit Peter Spiegel) 2008: *Unternimm Dein Leben. Als Lebensunternehmer zu neuem Erfolg*. Carl Hanser Verlag, München

Ridderstråle, Jonas/Nordström, Kjell A. 1999: F*unky Business – Talent Makes Capital Dance*. Bookhouse

Ripsas, Sven 1997: *Entrepreneurship als ökonomischer Prozeß: Perspektiven zur Förderung unternehmerischen Handelns*. Deutscher Universitäts-Verlag, Wiesbaden

Ripsas, Sven/Zumholz, Holger/Kolata, Christian 2007: "Strategische Planungsqualität, formale Businessplanung und Unternehmenserfolg – eine empirische Untersuchung der Gewinner von Businessplan-Wettbewerben". Beitrag zum FGF-Forum, Aachen

Roddick, Anita 1991: *Body and Soul.* Ebury Press, first edition

Röpke, Jochen 2002: *Der lernende Unternehmer: zur Evolution und Konstruktion unternehmerischer Kompetenz.* Mafex-Publikationen, Marburg

Rubin, Ron/Stuart, Avery G. 2001: *Success at Life: How to Catch and Live Your Dream.* New Market Press, New York

Sarasvathy, Saras D. 2009: *Effectuation: Elements of Entrepreneurial Expertise* (New Horizons in Entrepreneurship), Edward Elgar Publishing Ltd., Cheltenham

Schumpeter, Joseph 1983 *The Theory of Economic Development: An Inquiry Into Profits, Capital, Credit, Interest, and the Business Cycle* (Social Science Classics Series), Transaction Publ

Sloterdijk, Peter 2005: *Im Weltinnenraum des Kapitals.* Suhrkamp Verlag, Frankfurt am Main

De Soto, Hernando 2003: *The Mystery of Capital: Why Capitalism Triumphs in the West and Fails Everywhere Else.* Basic Books, New York

Spiegel, Peter 2007: *Muhammad Yunus – Banker der Armen.* Herder Verlag, Freiburg im Breisgau

Stähler, Patrick 2002: *Geschäftsmodelle in der digitalen Ökonomie: Merkmale, Strategien und Auswirkungen.* Electronic Commerce, Bd. 7. Josef Eul Verlag, Köln

Sternberg, Rolf/Brixy, Udo/Schlapfner, Jan-Florian 2006: *Länderbericht Deutschland 2005.* Global Entrepreneurship Monitor, Hannover/Nürnberg

Suter, Martin 2002: *Business Class. Geschichten aus der Welt des Managements.* Diogenes Verlag, Zürich

Szyperski, Norbert 2004: "Künstler und Unternehmer. Was können Wissenschaftler von ihnen lernen?" In: *DBW Editorial* 04/2004

Timmons, Jeffry 1994: *New Venture Creation. Entrepreneurship for the 21st Century.* 4. Auflage, Irwin, Boston

Timmons, Jeffry/Spinelli, Steven/Zacharakis, Andrew 2004: *Business plans that work.* McGraw-Hill Professional, New York

Vesper, Karl 1993: *New Venture Mechanics.* Prentice Hall, Englewood Cliffs, N.J.

Volkmann, Christine K./Tokarski, Kim Oliver 2006: *Entrepreneurship. Gründung und Wachstum von jungen Unternehmen.* Lucius & Lucius, Stuttgart

Witt, Peter 2005: *Stand und offene Fragen der Gründungsforschung.* Studie für das Bundesministerium für Bildung und Forschung (BMBF), Vallendar ZDF/FWU Institut für Film und Bild in Wissenschaft und Unterricht 2004/2005: *Mission X: Der Kampf um die schwarze Formel.* Mainz

About the author

Guenter Faltin is Professor of Entrepreneurship at the Free University of Berlin.

In 1985, Faltin started the Teekampagne ("tea campaign"), a venture that turned the German tea market upside down by betting on consumer education, transparency and traceability. Today, the company is the largest importer of Darjeeling world-wide.

Faltin initiated the Berlin-based "Entrepreneurship Lab" and has been a business angel for successful startups. Through the Faltin Foundation for Entrepreneurship, he promotes a new culture of entrepreneurship in Germany. In the United States, the Price-Babson Foundation recognized him with an award "for bringing entrepreneurial vitality to academe." In 2009, he won the German Founder's Award, as well as an award from Germany's Federal Ministry for Economics and Technology for his idea of "founding with components." In 2010 he received the Federal Cross of Merit from the German president for his pioneer work on entrepreneurship.

Acknowledgments

Writing a book is actually related to entrepreneurship. At the beginning is the initial idea: that the subject of starting up a company, as an act of active participation in economic life, should be recognized for its fundamental societal significance, but that this process must be approached quite differently from how it was done in the past. At universities, ideas grow through teaching and research, whereas in a start-up they grow primarily through hands-on practice – an endeavor through which you can easily lose your reputation as well as your own fortune. I remember a well-meaning colleague who urgently tried to dissuade me from starting up a company. According to him, a university professor was simply not up to the task.

My special thanks go to my long-time colleagues, associates and discussion partners, especially to Fritz Fleischmann for our many animated exchanges on the socio-political significance of this subject as the logical "second stage of the Enlightenment"; to Sven Ripsas for our joint efforts to bridge the gap between business administration and entrepreneurship, our discussions of the value of business plan competitions and the idea of concept-creative start-ups; to Dietrich Winterhager for his patience and forbearance in the face of my criticisms of our own discipline; to Frithjof Bergmann for contact and insight into the most up-to-date technology like the digital fabricator; to Jürgen Zimmer for our memorable and intense experiences – and not just with the "Adventure Restaurant"; to Otto Herz for our heated discussions on whether our educational system contributes to entrepreneurship or not; to Stephan Reimertz for his valuable suggestions from the worlds of art and history; to Peter Spiegel, Kurt Hammer, Ullrich Boehm, Hartmut Frech and Hans Luther for their insightful and sustained support.

As it turned out, I quickly found discussion partners who were familiar with the subject from an international perspective and who encouraged me: people like Miroslaw Malek (Humboldt University, Berlin), the late Jeffry Timmons, William

Bygrave (both of Babson College), Allan Gibb (Durham), Howard Stevenson (Harvard), Eric van Hippel (MIT) and Seri Phongphit (Chulalongkorn). I had the good fortune to experience Ivan Illich (who called to my attention Aristotle's classification of common fraud, prostitution and commerce as deadly sins); to be in contact with Hernando de Soto, to conduct a workshop with Muhammad Yunus and later to experience micro-entrepreneurship on site in Bangladesh.

Many of my friends and colleagues have followed the progress of these ideas with insight and good will. For their constructive criticism, I wish to thank Walter Dürr, Günther Seliger, Volker Trommsdorf, Hans Georg Gemünden, Professor Ann-Kristin Achleitner, Heinz Klandt, Professor Ulrich Braukmann, Professor Reza Asghari, Georg Schreyögg, Dieter Puchta, Helge Löbler, Andreas Gebhardt, Eberhard Wagemann, Matthias Horx, Liv Kirsten Jacobsen, Katrin Fischer, Dieter Kleiber, Gerd Hoff, Dieter Geulen, Gerhard Huhn, Peter Goebel, Maritta Koch-Weser, Johanna Richter, Ralf Fücks, Holm Friebe, George White, Gunter Pauli, Wolfgang Sachs, Harry Hermanns, Mike Schluroff, Klaus Heymann, Eike Gebhardt, Peter Schweizer, Johannes Linner, Hannes Offenbacher, Markus Strauch, Patrik Varadinek, Dorothea Kress, Utz Paul Karpenstein, Winfried Kretschmer, David Krahlisch, Udo Blum, Alf Ammon, Franz Dullinger, Stefan Becker, Ulrike Becker, Marie-Therese Albert, Angelika Krüger and Christine Lipp-Peetz.

I thank all the business founders in my innermost circle for accepting the challenge of putting the principles described in this book to the test, especially Holger Johnson, who with his ebuero validated most impressively the principle of "function, not convention," as well as Rafael Kugel with RatioDrink, Conrad Bölicke, Thomas Fuhlrott, Max Senges, Thorsten Alles, Thomas Klamroth, Thomas Wachsmuth, Viktoria Trosien, Caveh Valipour Zonooz, Katja Birkenbach, Christian Fenner, Nils Dreyer, Thomas Strassburg and Stefan Arndt, all with their own start-ups.

Representing all those at the Laboratory for Entrepreneurship who discussed their ideas with me and so helped to direct the focus to the essentials are Lars Hinrichs, Lukasz Gadowski, David Diallo, Michel Aloui, Hans Reitz, Jeanette Griesel, Ron Hillmann, Michael Silberberger and Ehssan Dariani, just to name a few.

And of course there is the company, Projektwerkstatt, where it all began. My special thanks go to my long-time allies Peter Lange, Thomas Räuchle, Verena Heinrich, Shanti, Kathrin Gassert, as well as to Florian Komm, Jaroslaw Leszczynski, Verena Bischoff, Bozena Schymankiewitz, Simon Jochim and to the friends and business partners of the Projektwerkstatt: Helga Breuninger, Markus Hipp, Klaus Weidner, Leo Pröstler, Penelope Rosskopf, Alexander Wolf, Karl and Jwala Gamper, Karl Hacker, Helmut Spanner, Ashok Lohia, Ajay Kichlu, Anshuman Kanoria, Ashok Sengupta and Sujoy Srimal. My thanks also to sources of inspiration like Gabi van Dyk, Thomas Heinle, Hans Wall, Werner Wiesner, Johannes Dinnebier, Jana Dreikhausen and Otto Ulrich; to our partners at the Innovation Campus Wolfsburg represented by Oliver Syring, Margarete Hofmann and Maren Leinweber; to my colleagues from the Charité-Stiftung, Stefan Gutzeit and Friederike Hoffmann, as well as to the initiators of the Network for Teaching Entrepreneurship, Stephen Brenninkmeijer, Ferdinand Schneider, Kyra Prehn, and Connie and Wolf-Dieter Hasenclever.

I would like to express my profound gratitude to my assistant Barbara Hoppe, whose exceptional commitment was instrumental in the creation of this manuscript; to Stefanie Haric, in whose many formulations I found inspiring support; and to Gudrun Fabian and Nipawan Mandalay for their patience and understanding during the final stages of preparing this manuscript. And last, but not least I wish to thank Martin Janik, who was most charitable as he guided me through the complexities of the publishing process.

P.S.: If you think you're already too old to start a business, then please talk to our "youngest" founder, Bernhard Heising, 79 years of age. (Founding a start-up keeps you young!)

For further steps on the route to your own company

Take advantage of the publications and interviews with business founders at the Laboratory for Entrepreneurship.

They were produced specifically for this purpose and documented as templates for the individual work processes of each business founder. They are examples designed to help you systematically develop your own entrepreneurial design.

www.entrepreneurship.de.

Please register at this website to receive free information about the events sponsored by the Laboratory and the Stiftung Entrepreneurship.

Stiftung Entrepreneurship

The foundation was set up with capital and facilities provided by Dr. Guenter Faltin (80%) and Dr. Dietrich Winterhager (20%), Professors at the Free University of Berlin. Its aim is to foster a positive environment for the culture of entrepreneurship worldwide.

Entrepreneurship is a perspective on human activity that seeks to bring creativity and courage, imagination and initiative, to the tasks of starting and running business ventures and social organizations. Entrepreneurship offers an opportunity for unconventional ideas and views. It aims at achieving success through transcending established structures, and it attracts artists, mavericks and all those who formerly were marginal to the business world. The economic and cultural development of a society depends on business initiatives that apply economic, social and artistic creativity to existing problems. Entrepreneurship develops opportunities through a creative process.

Stiftung Entrepreneurship
The Art and Science of Entrepreneurship

www.entrepreneurship.de